It's a Yorkie Life
Adult Coloring Book
For the Love of Yorkies

It's a Yorkie Life

DEDICATION

To all Yorkie lovers, big and small.
And to the Yorkies that inspired it all: Mickey and Chloe,
and their best friends: Ezra and Jack.

CONTENTS

CROSS WEAVE PATTERNS

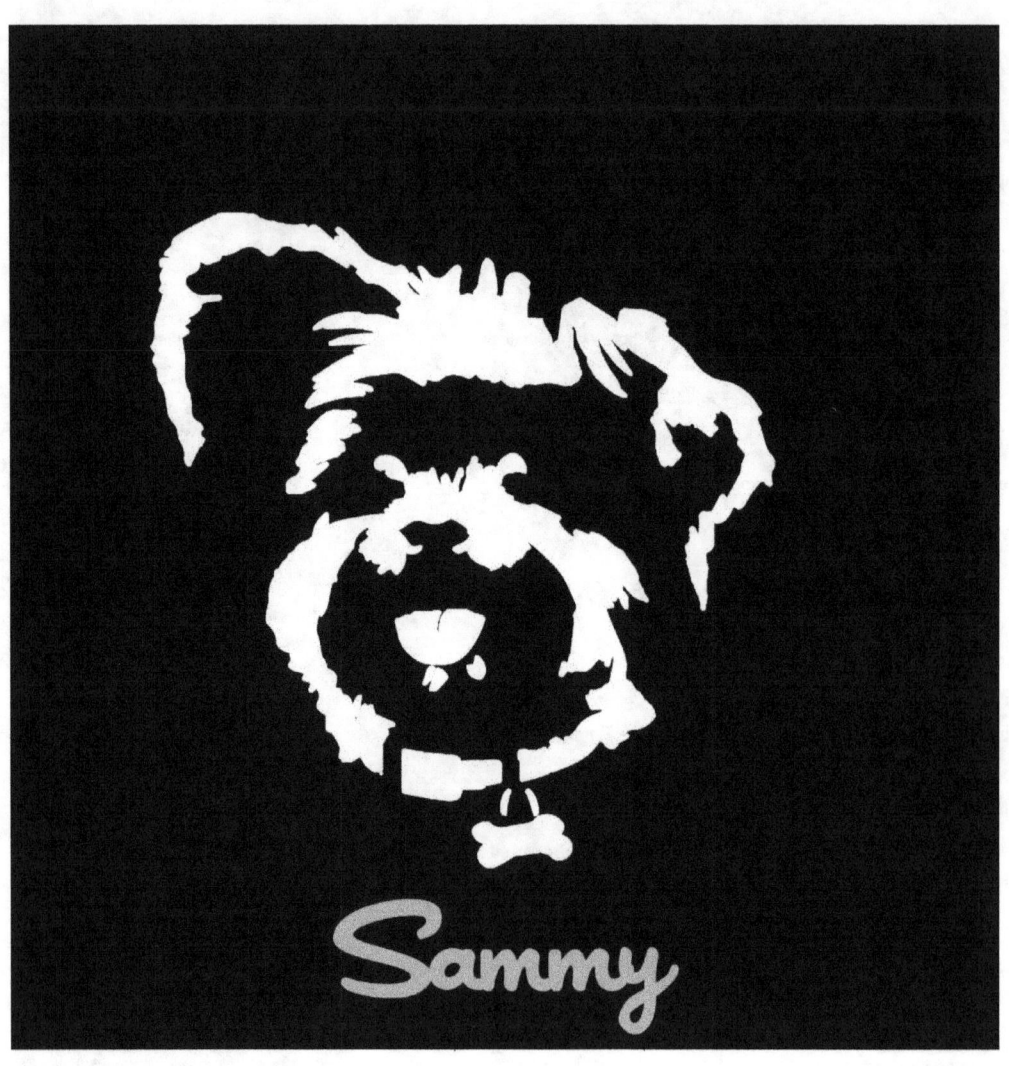

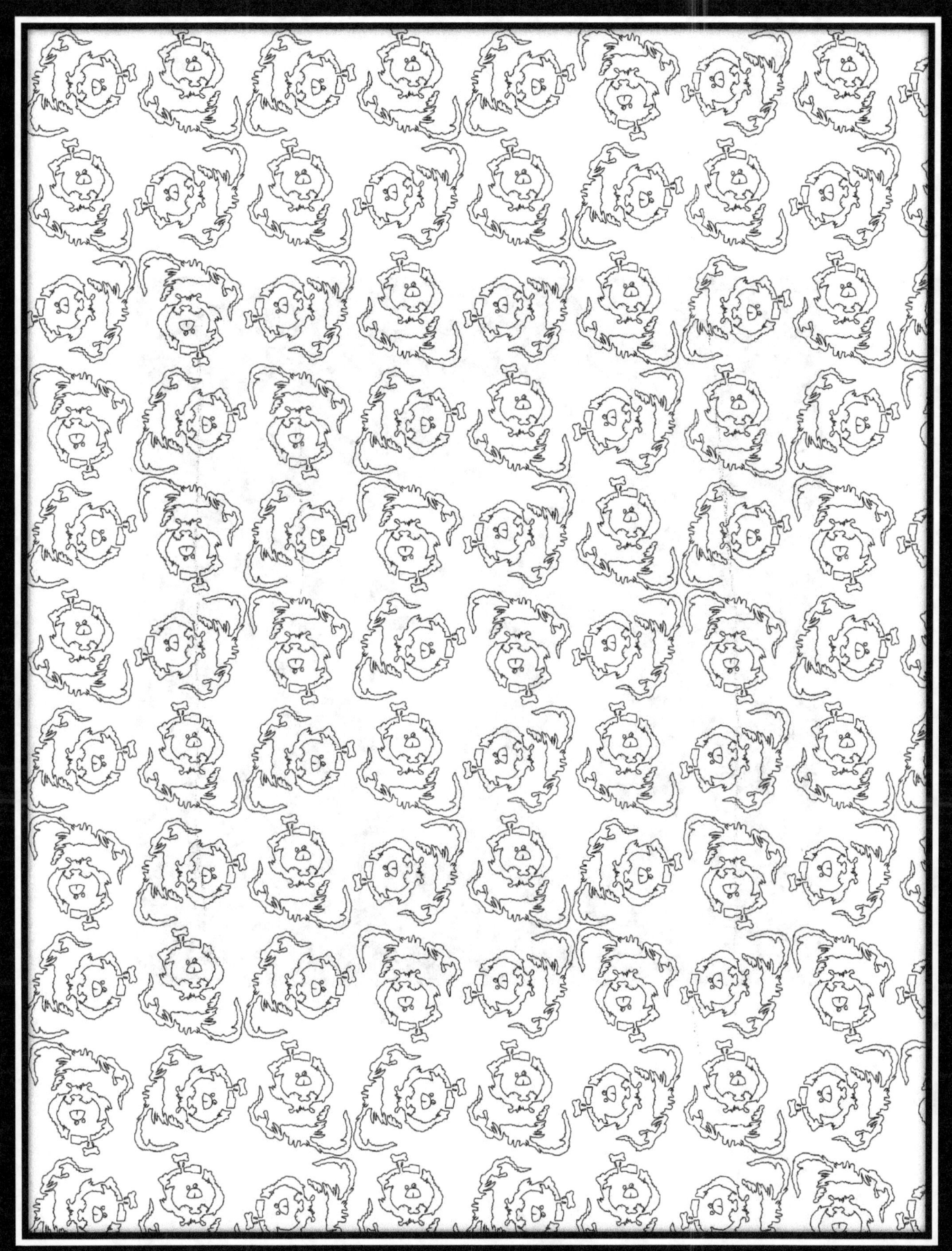

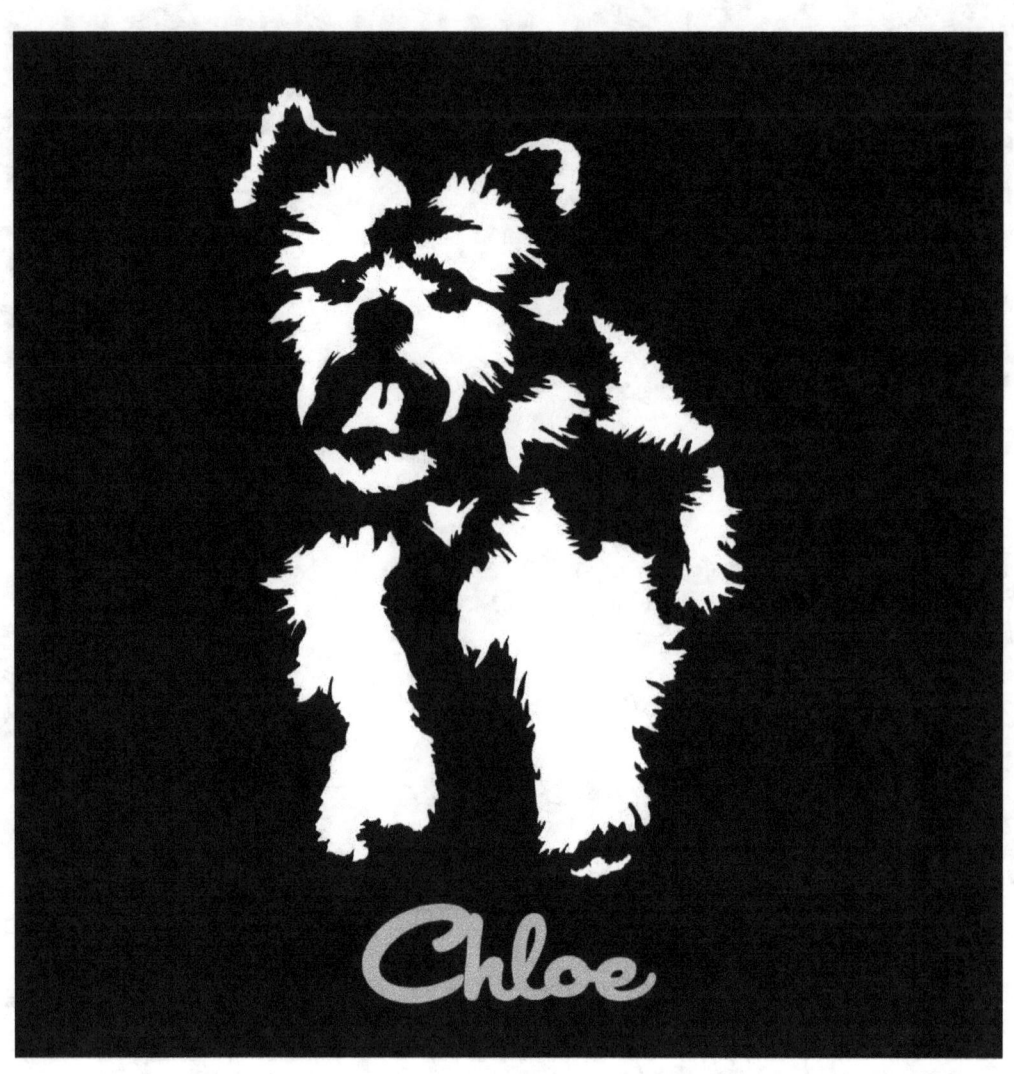

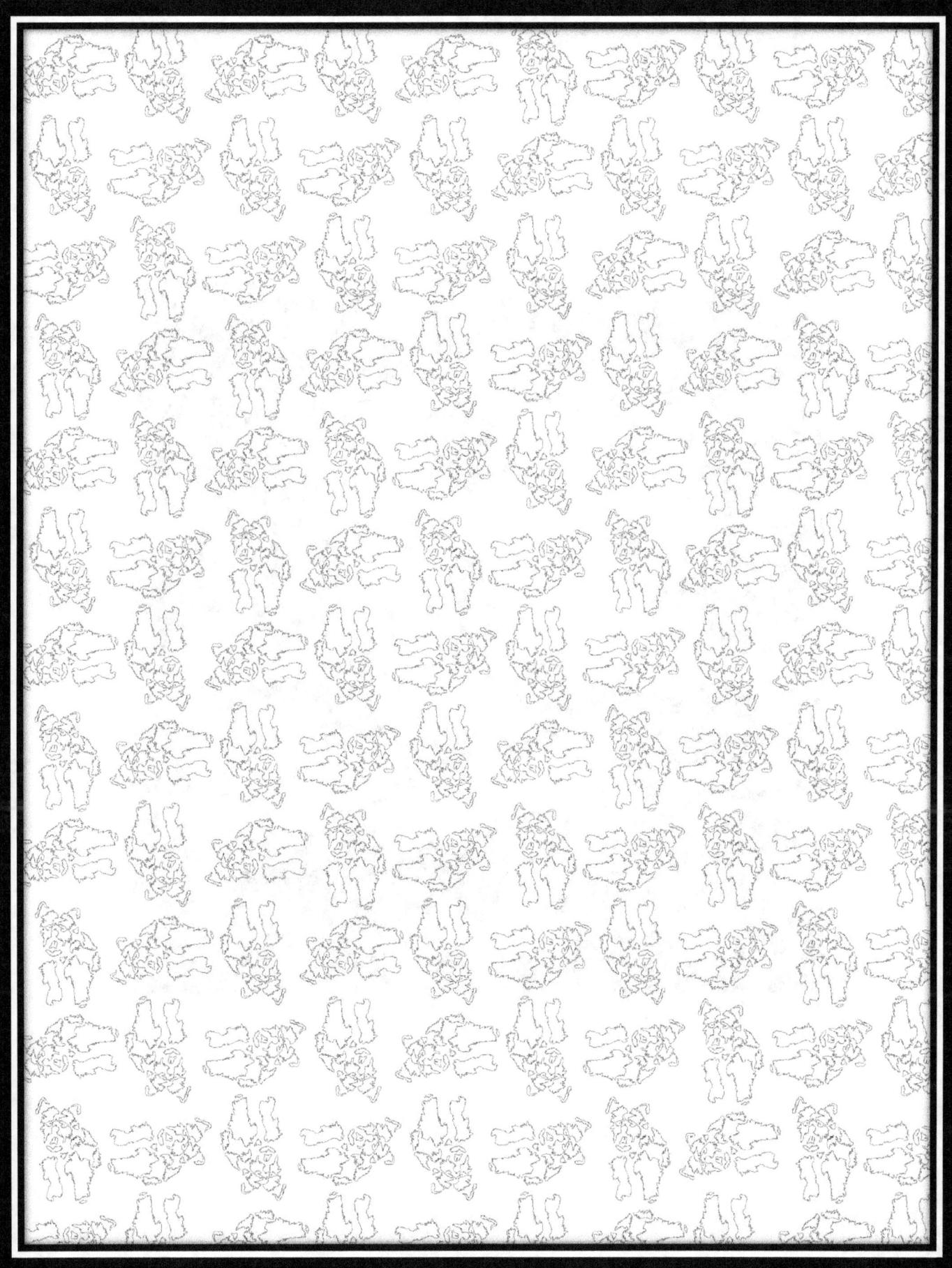

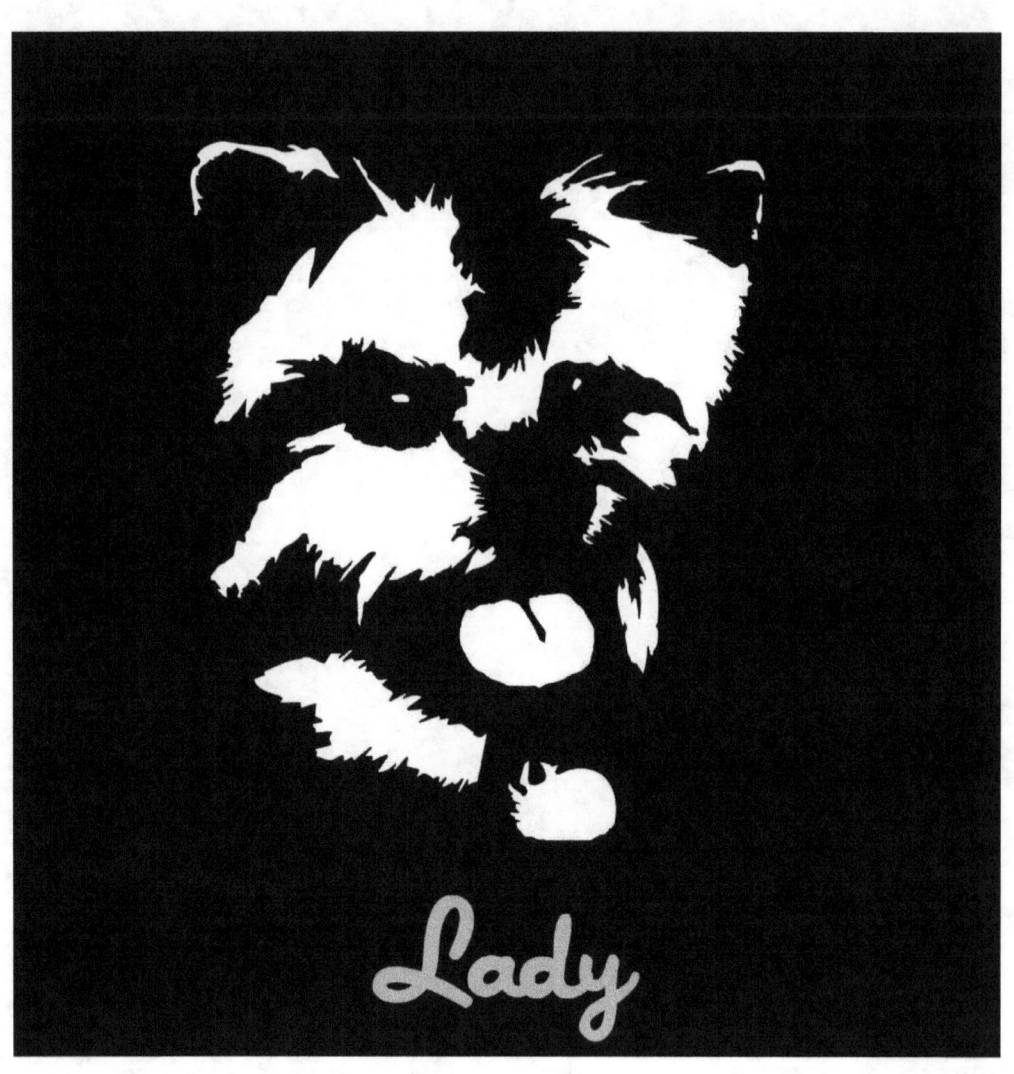

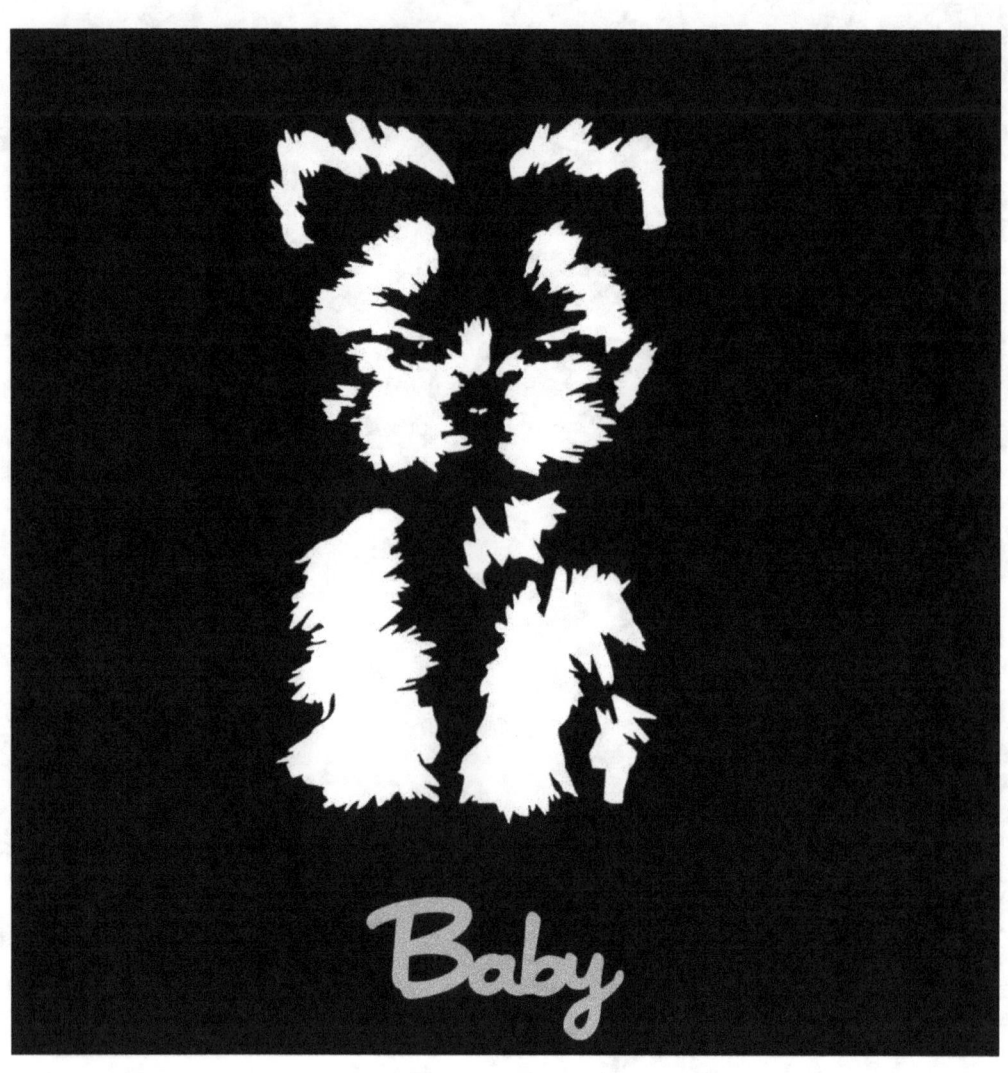

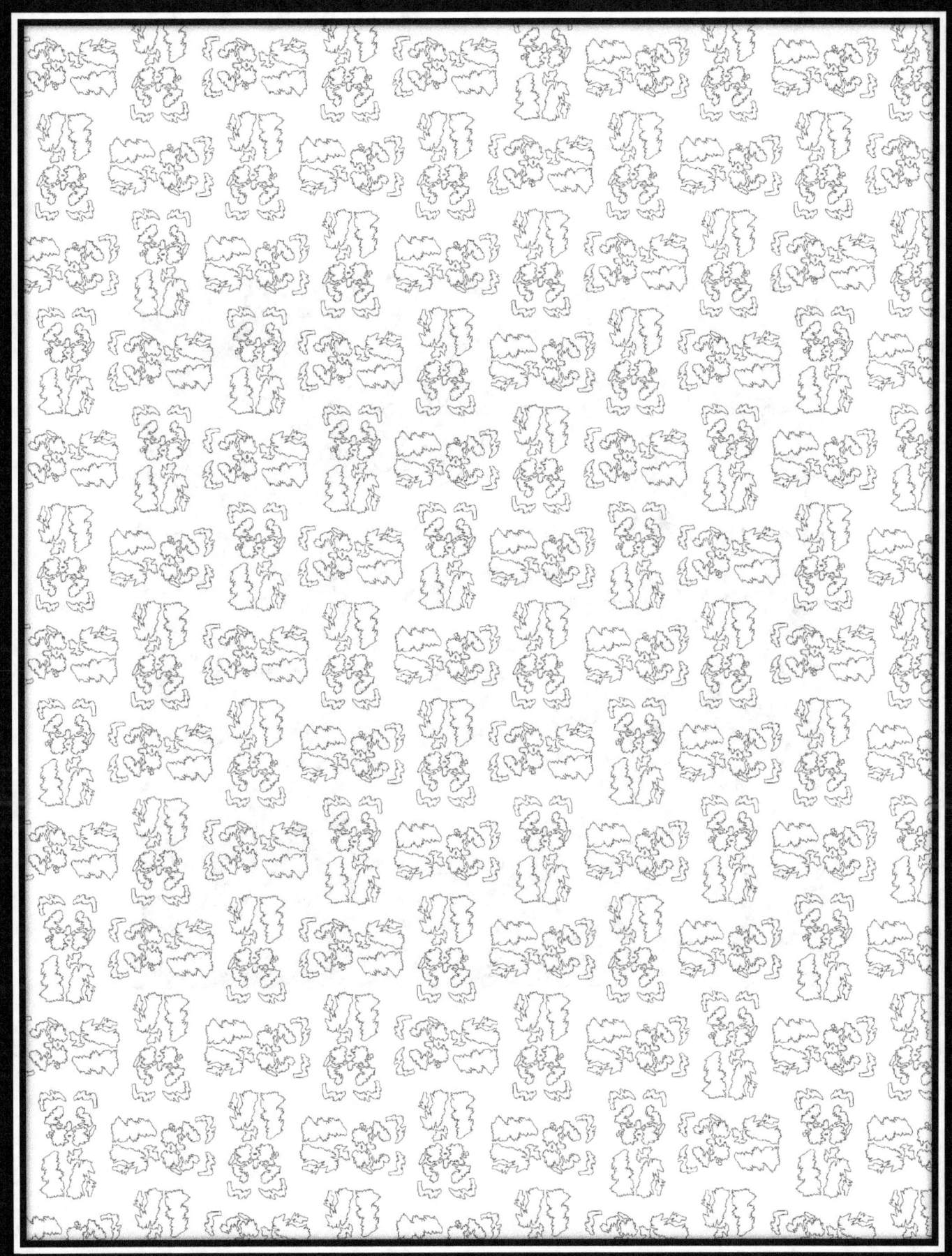

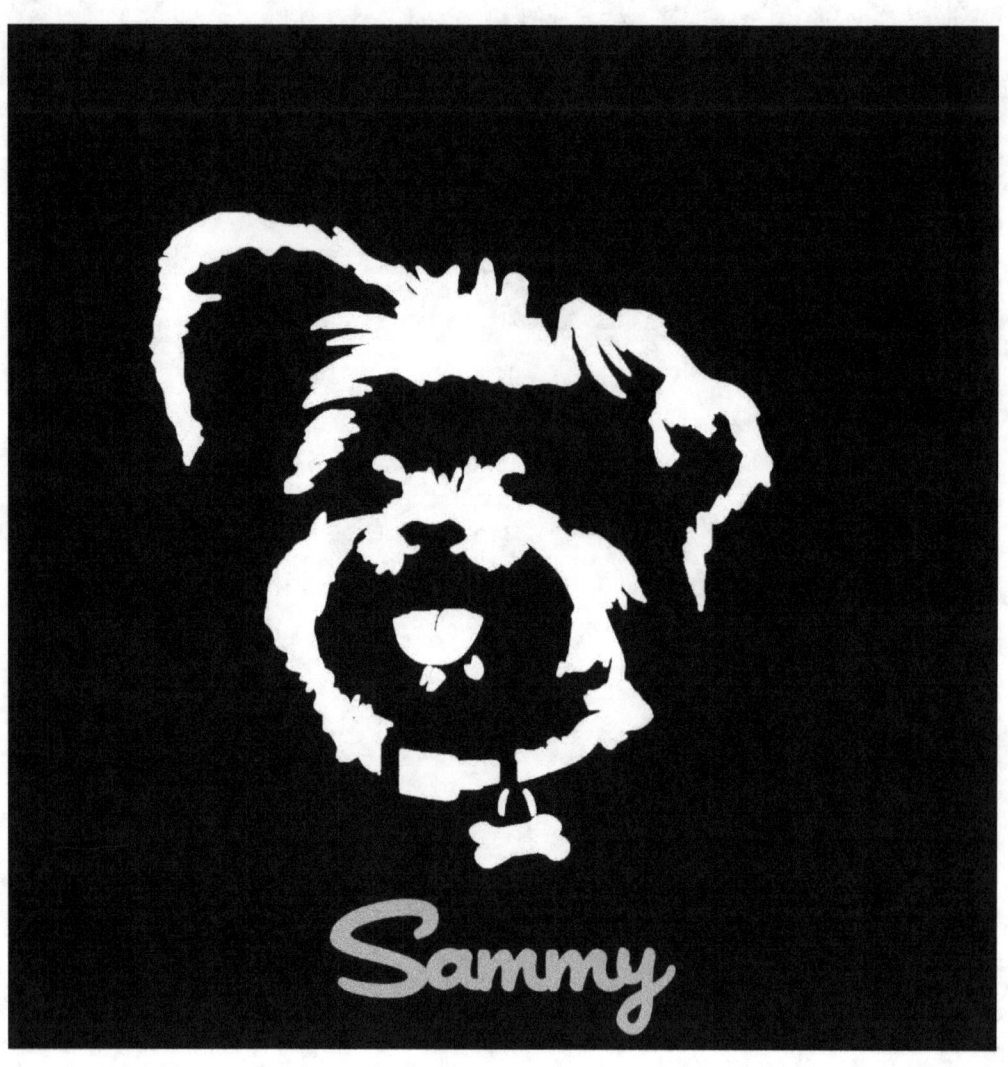

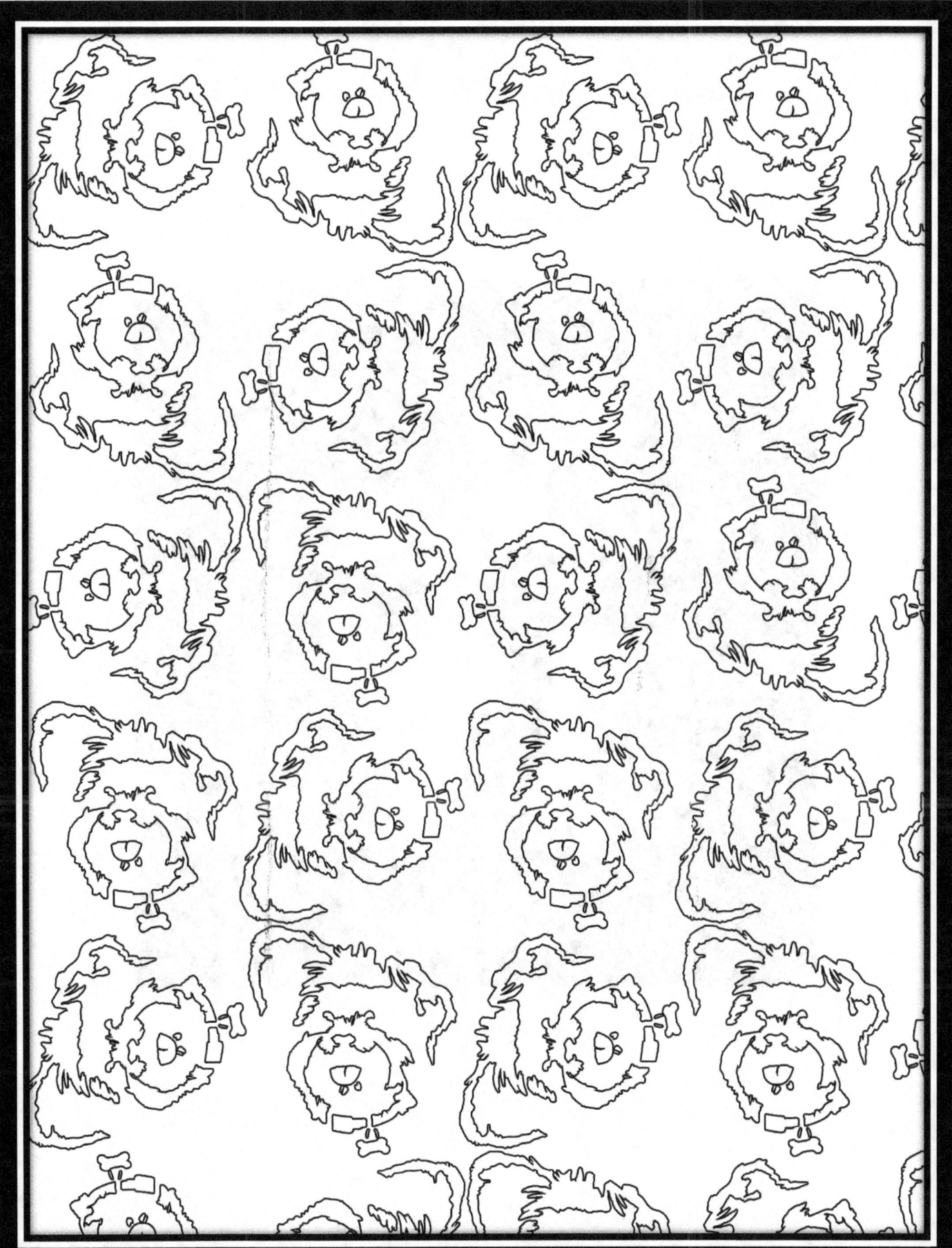

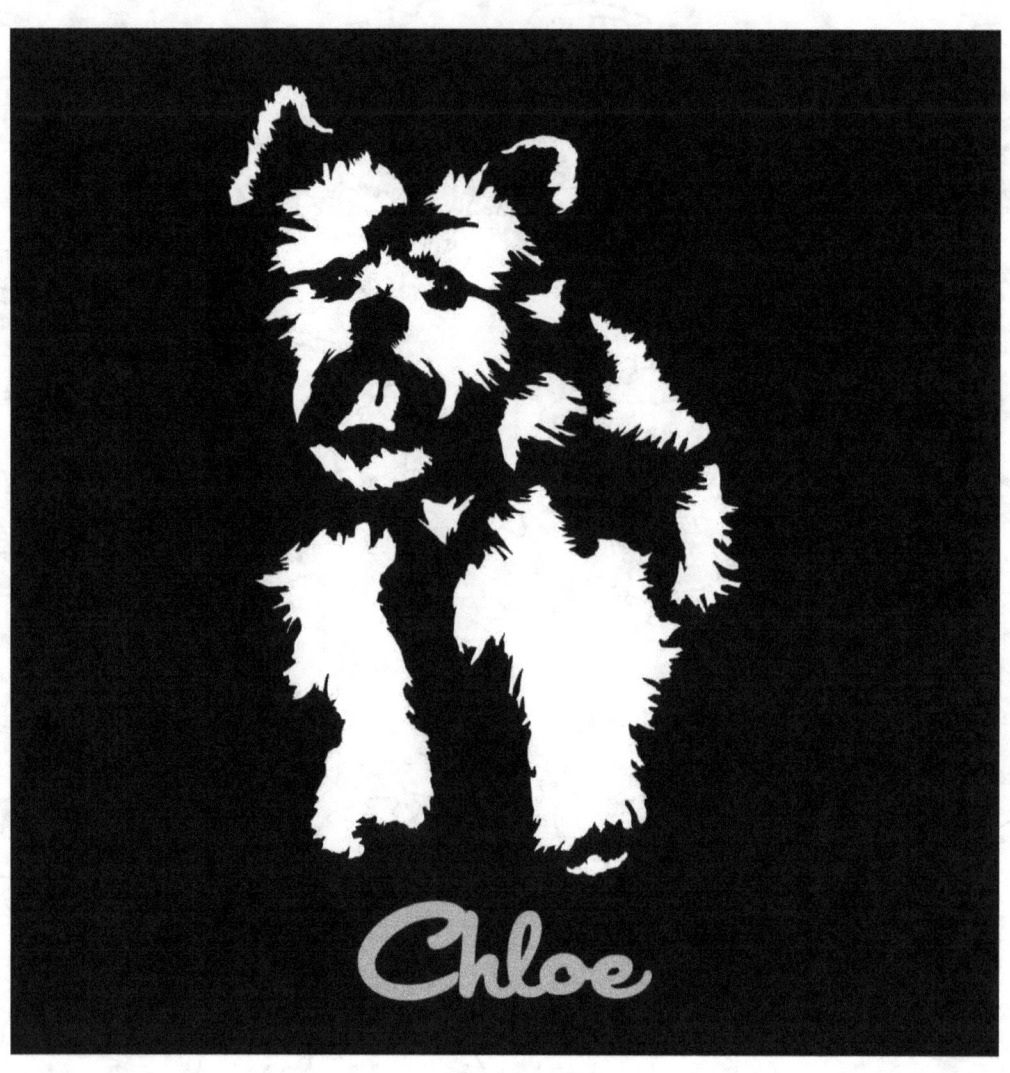

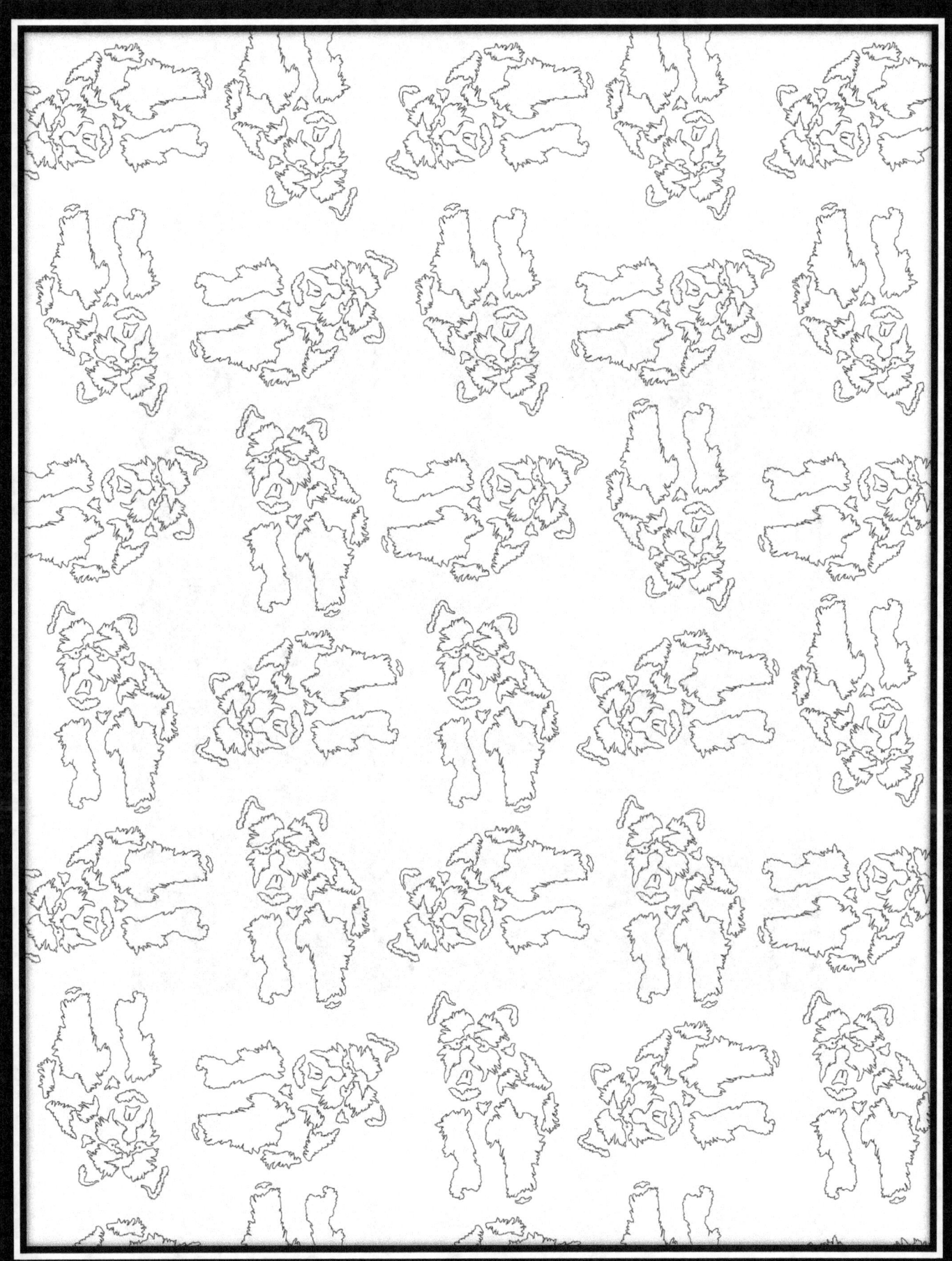

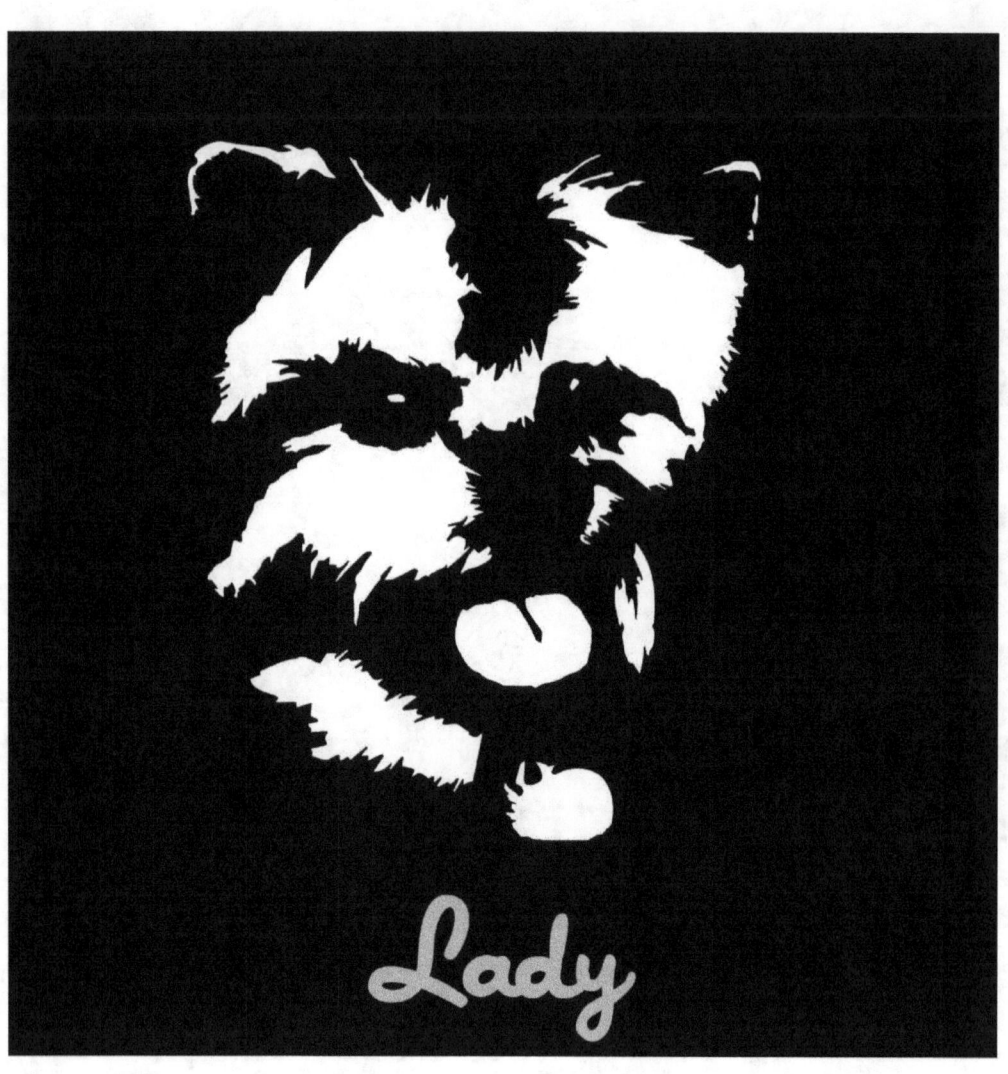

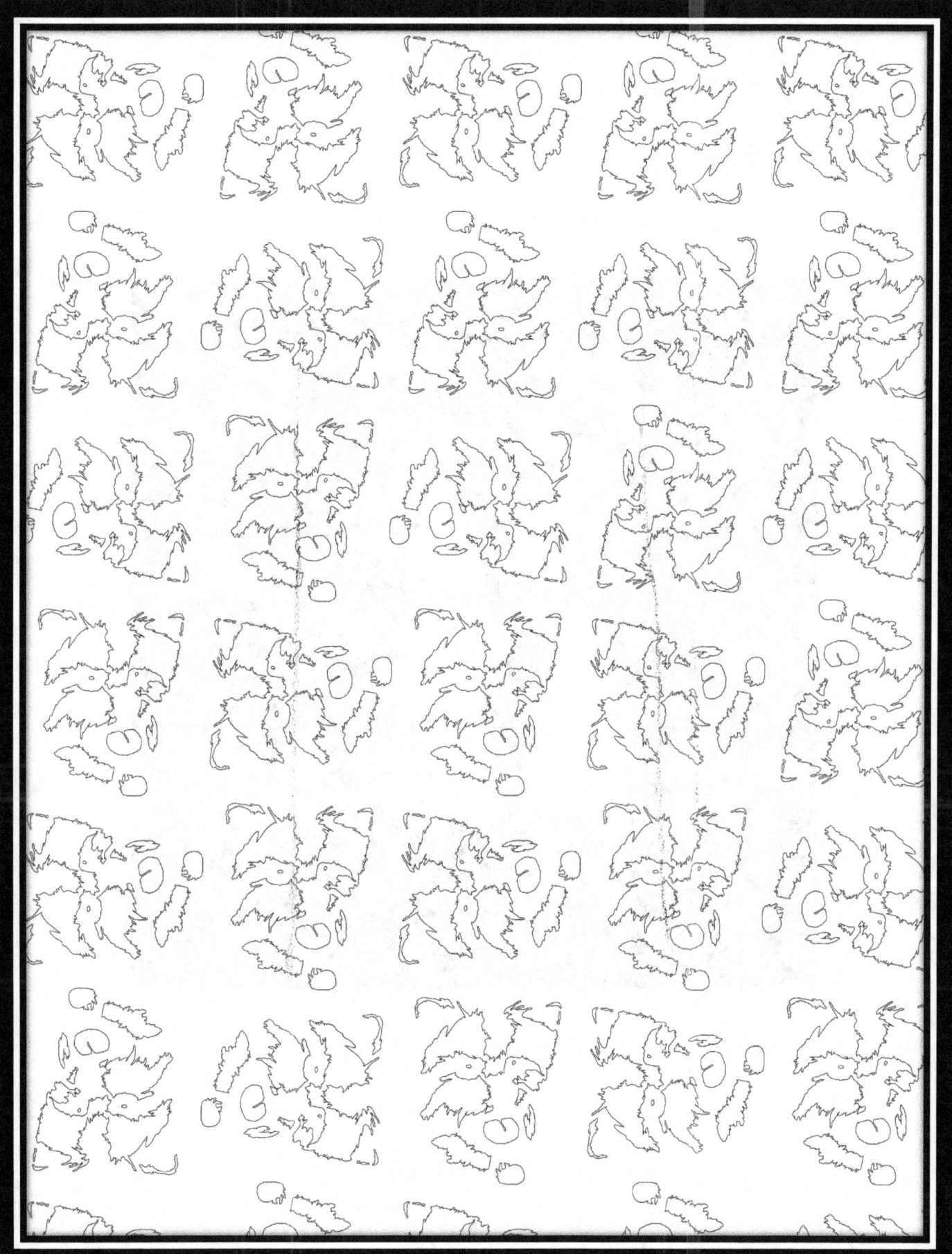

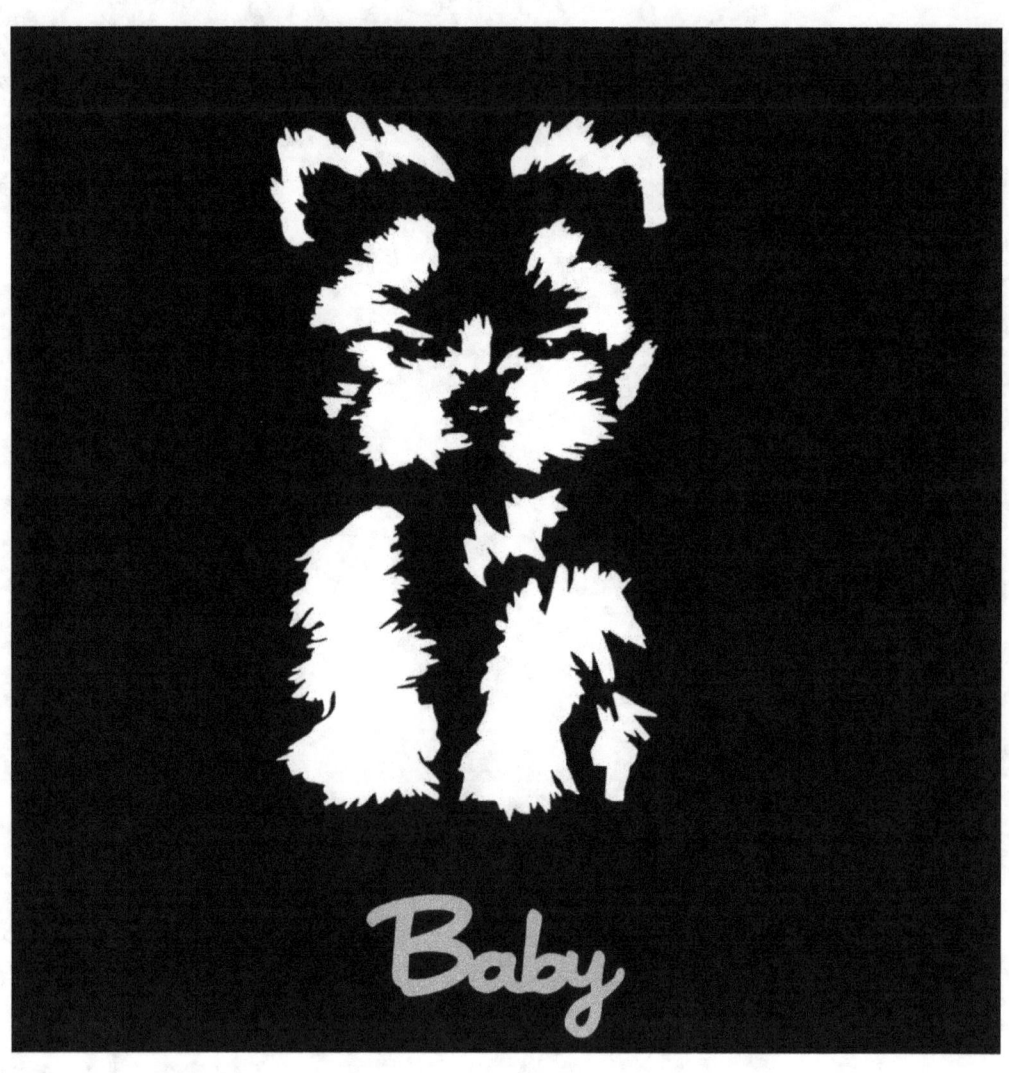

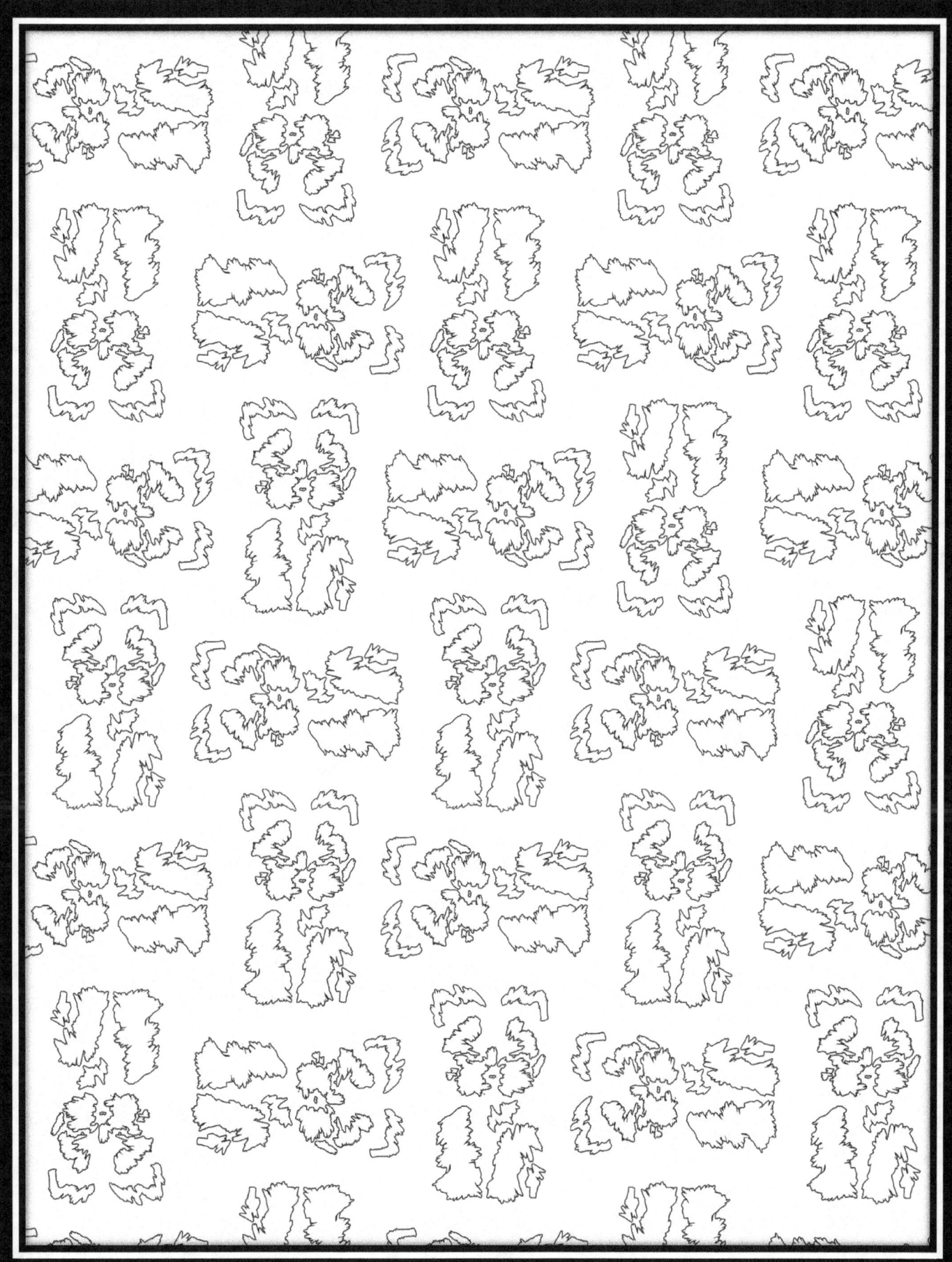

SPIRAL PATTERNS

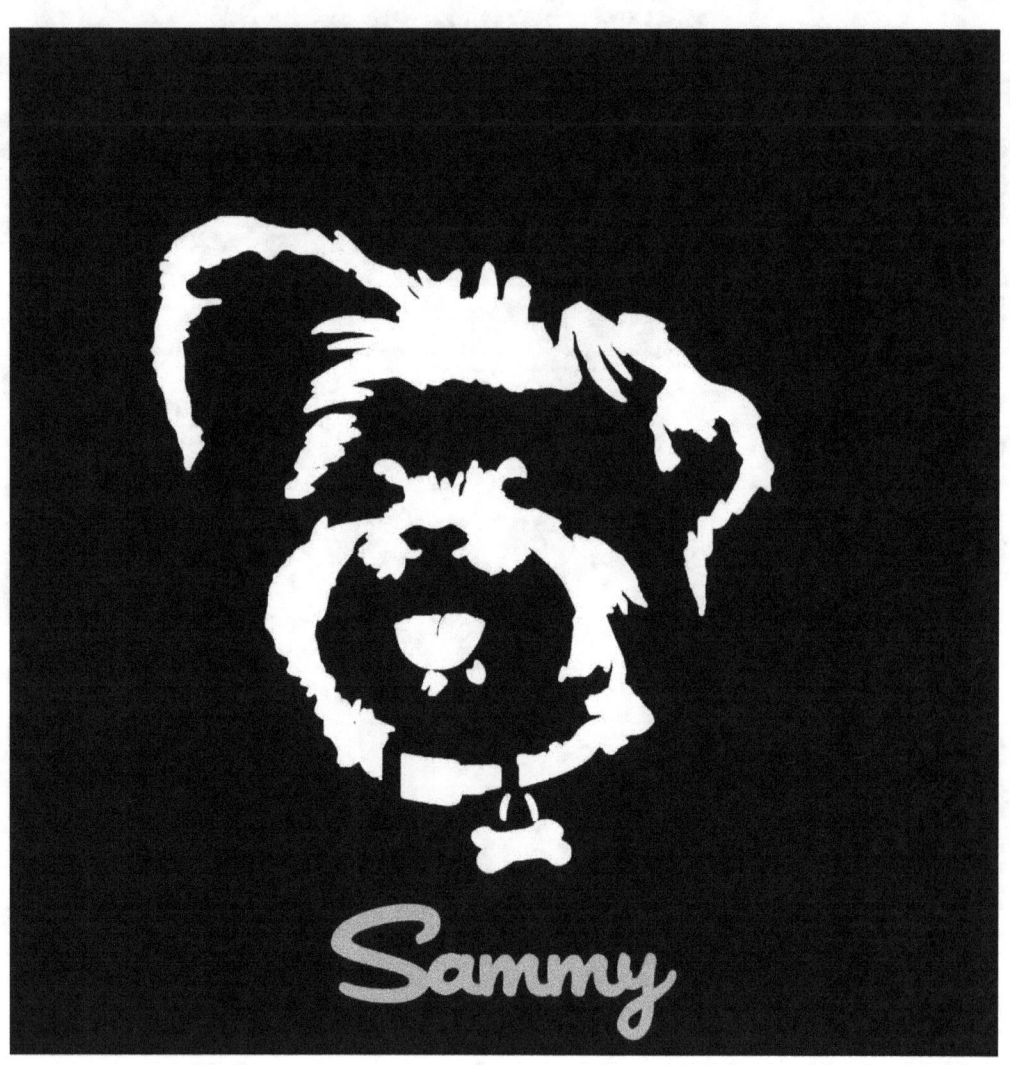

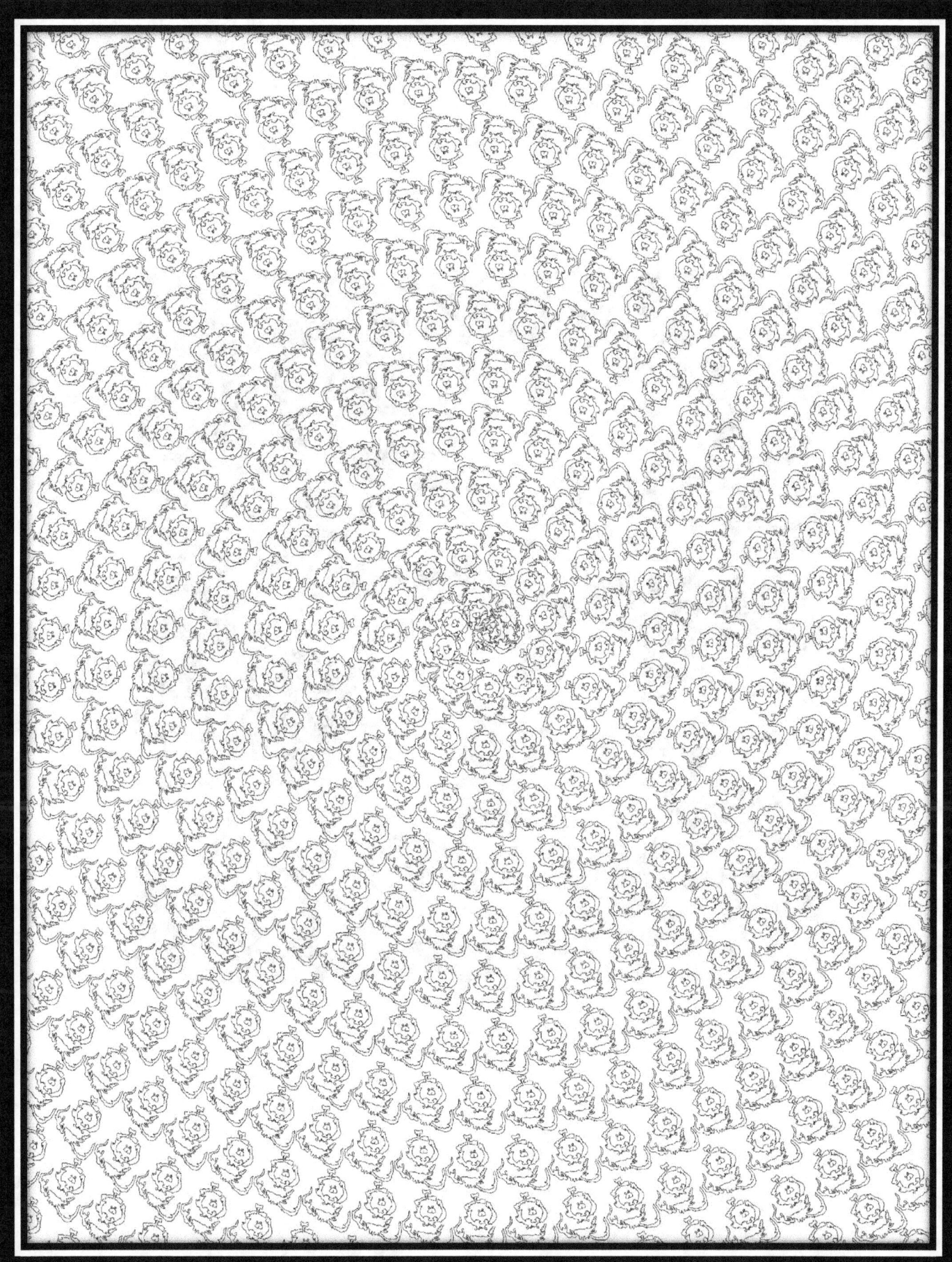

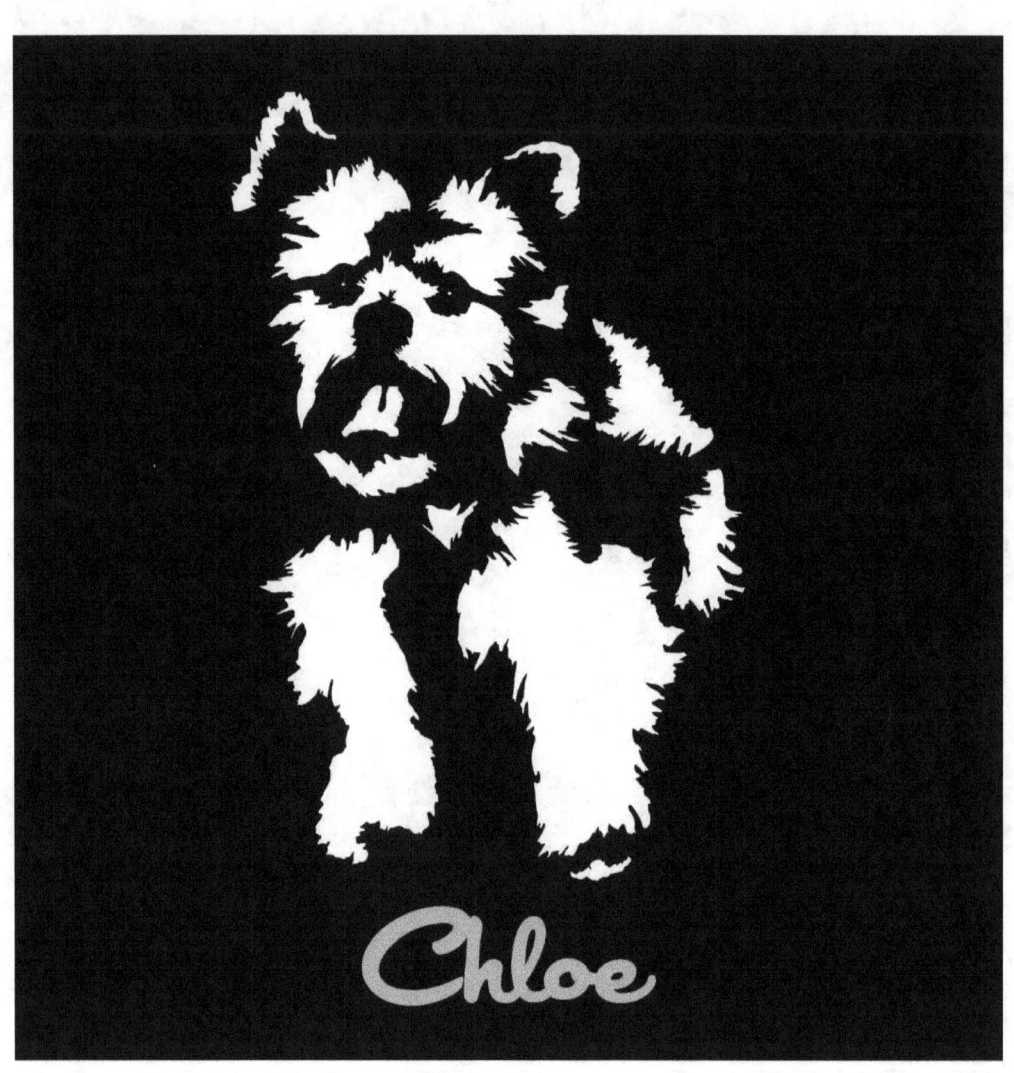

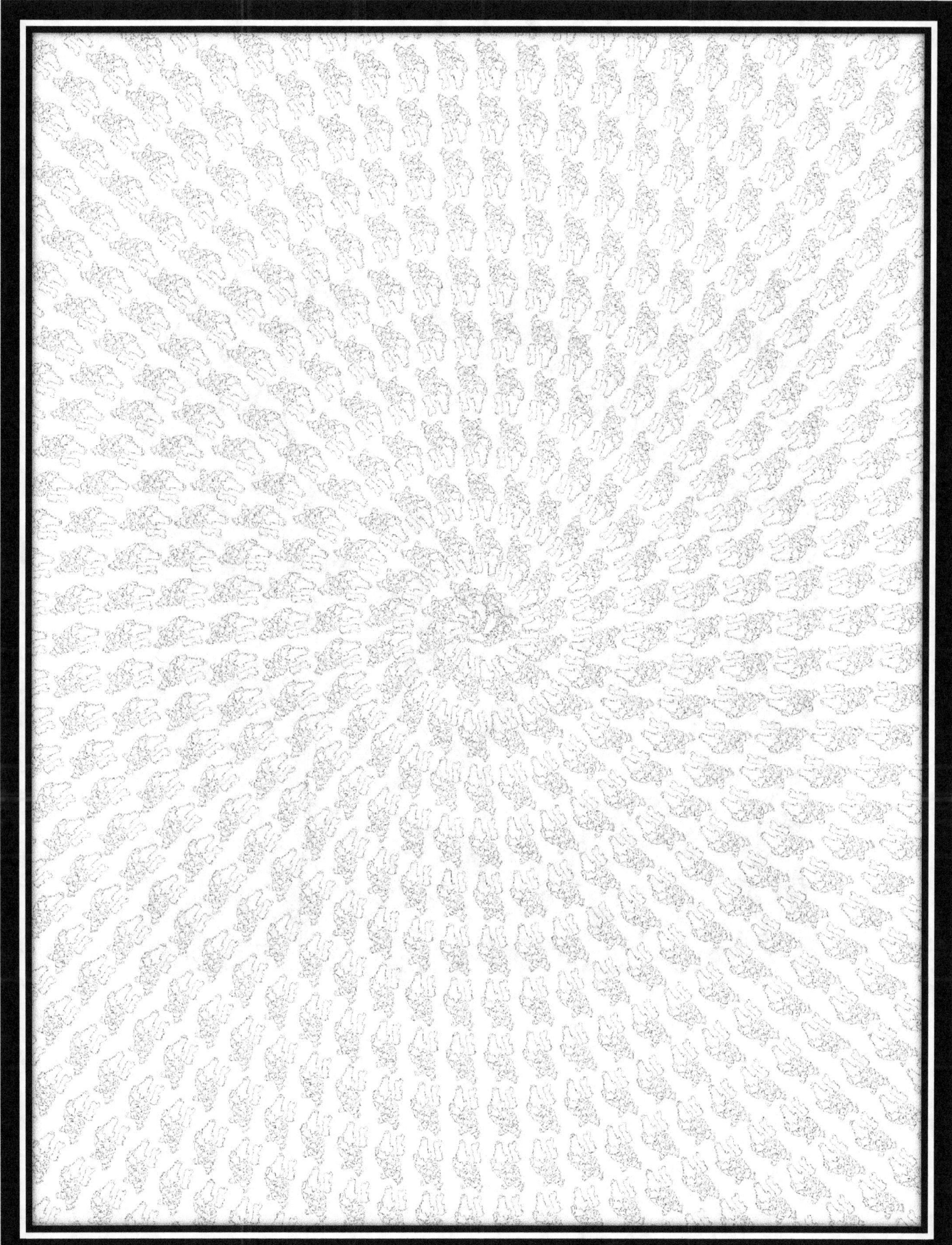

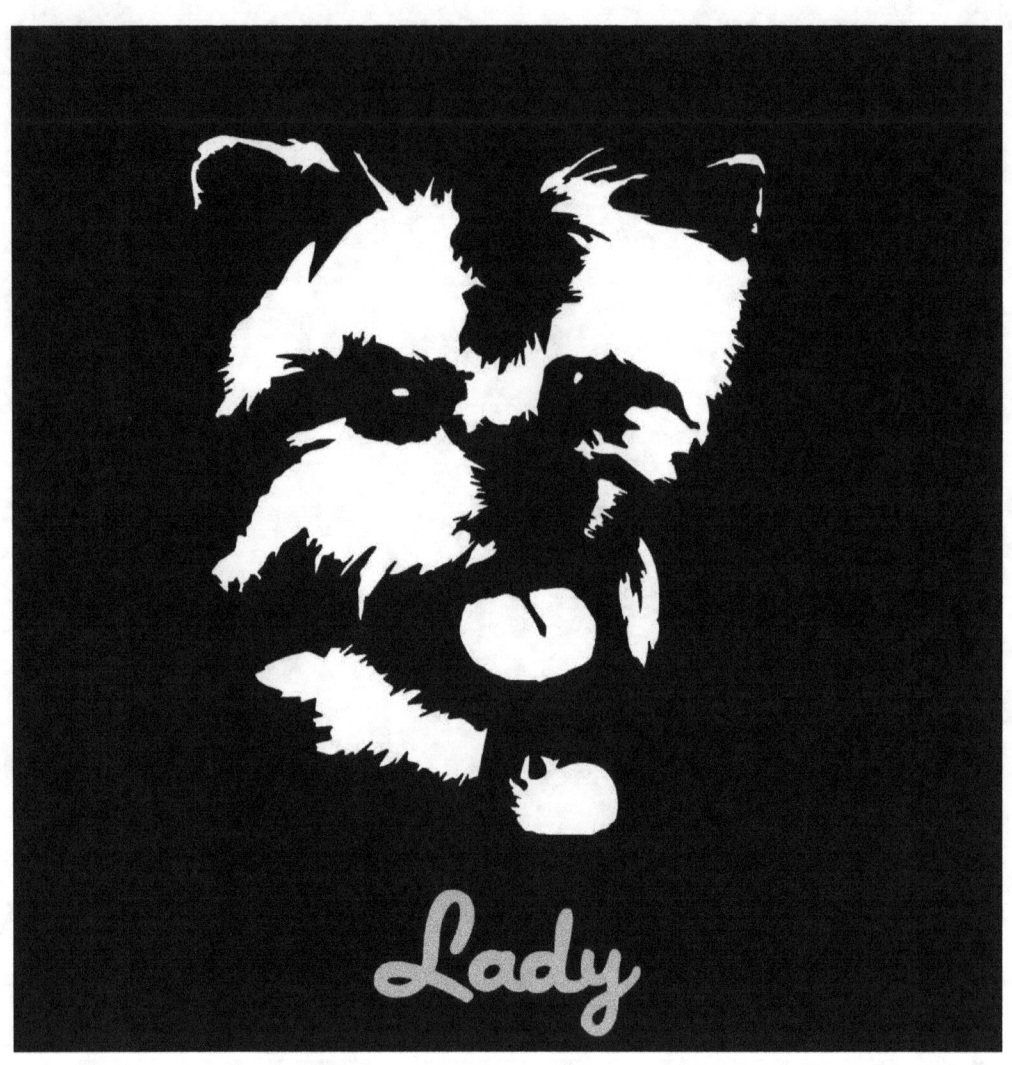

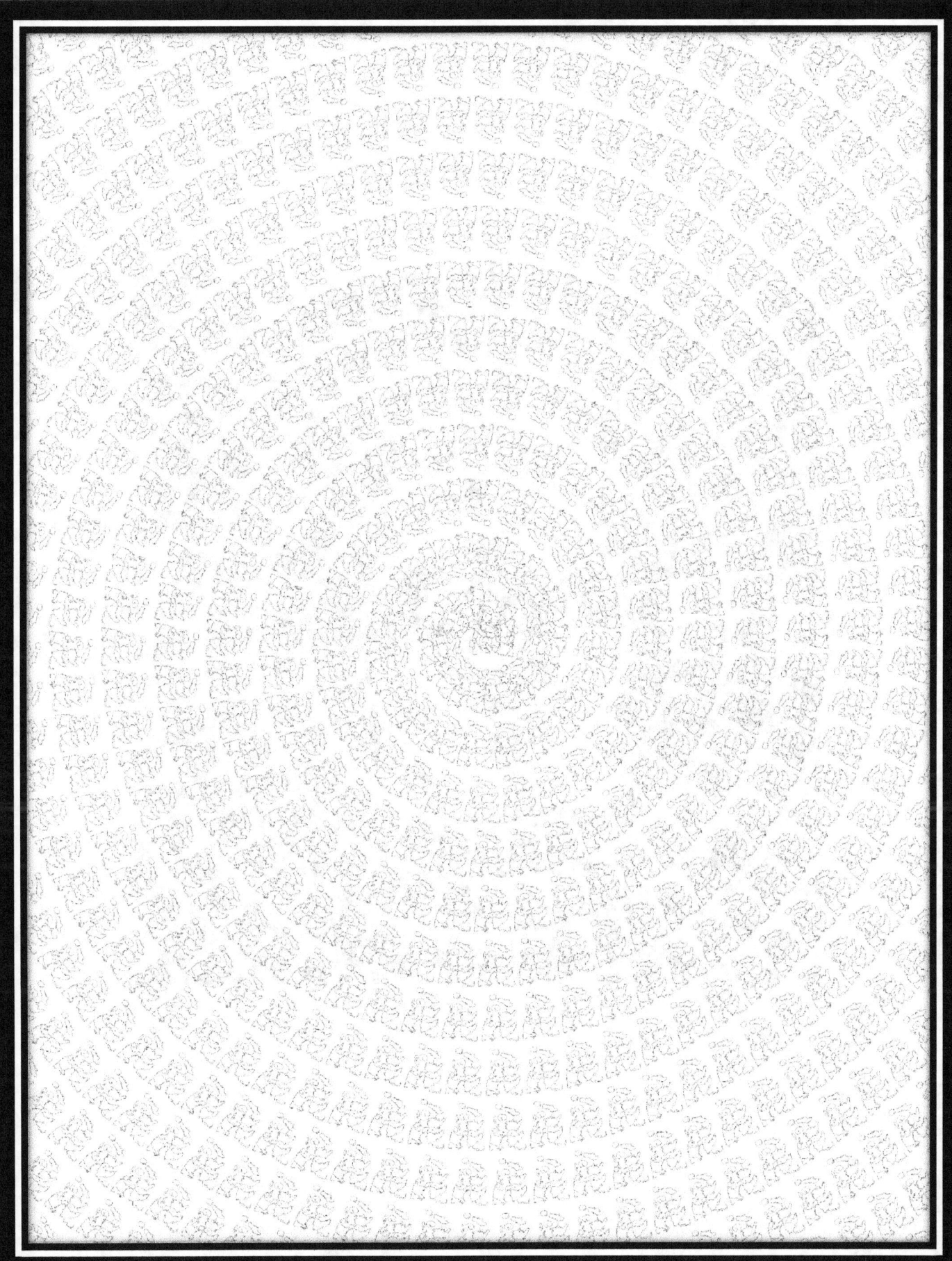

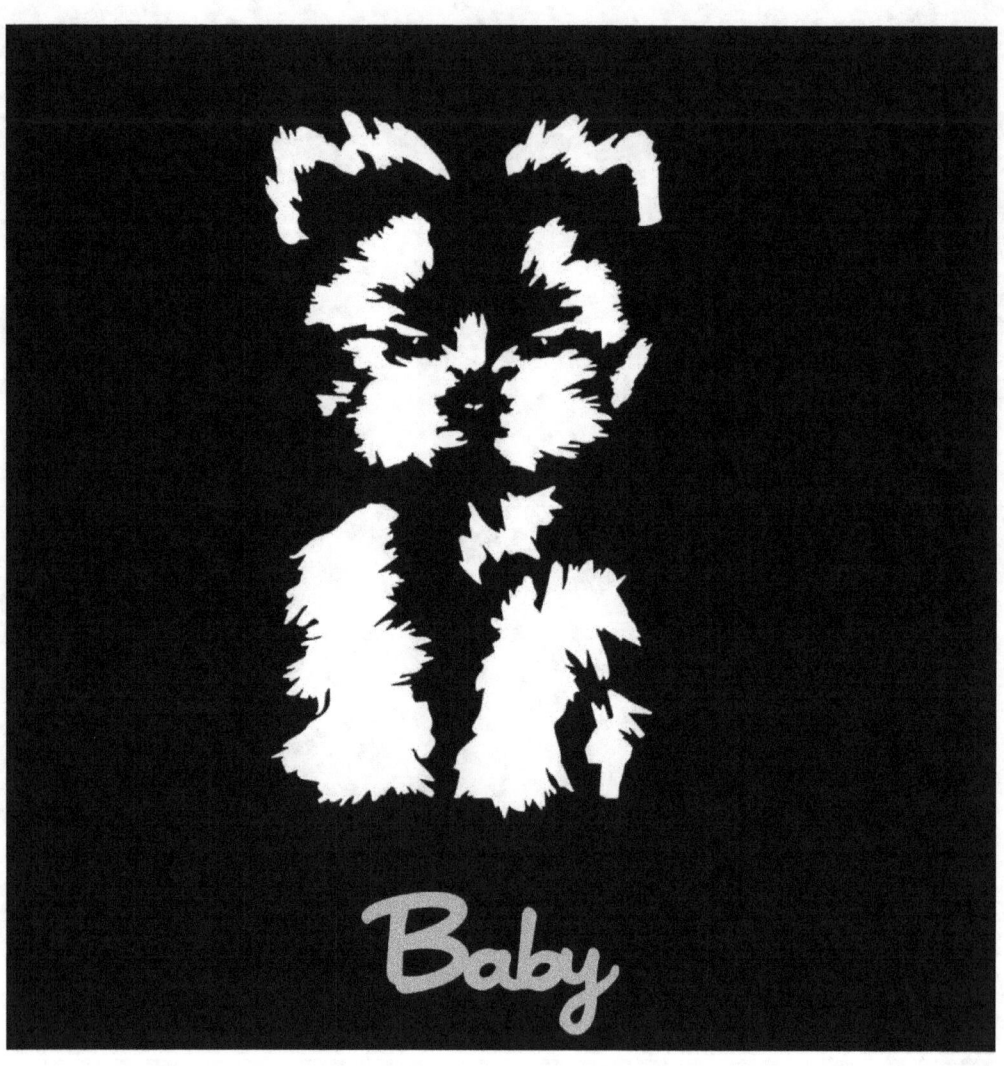

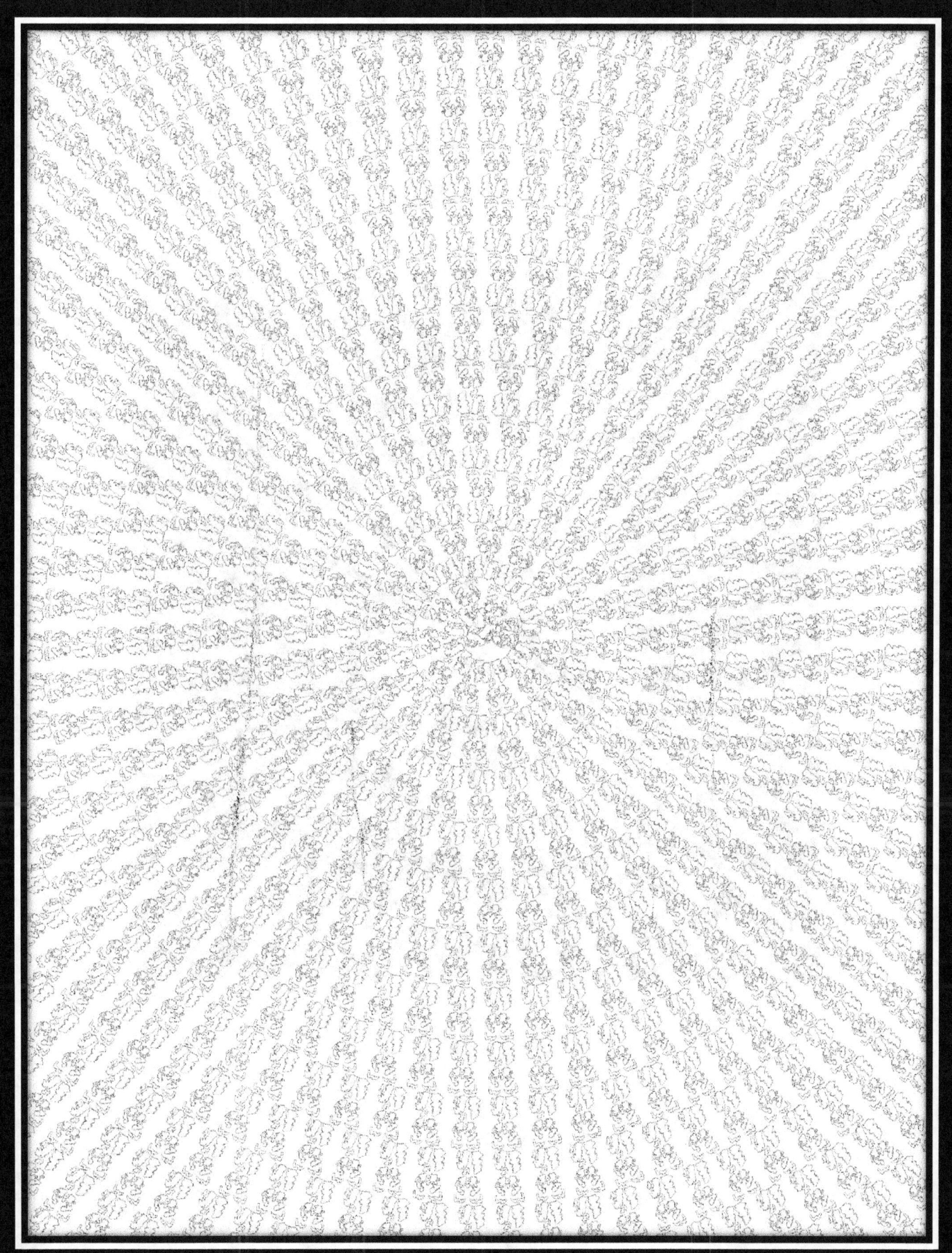

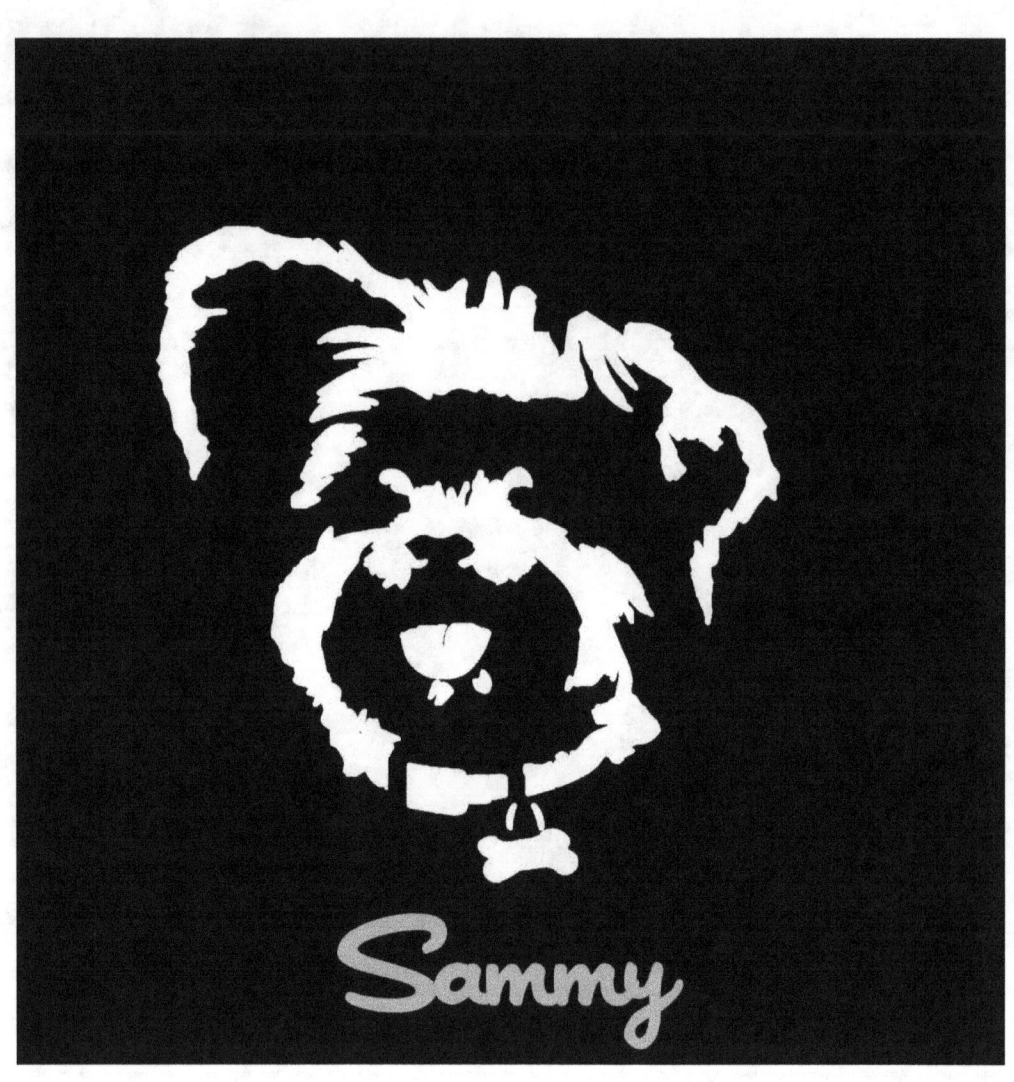

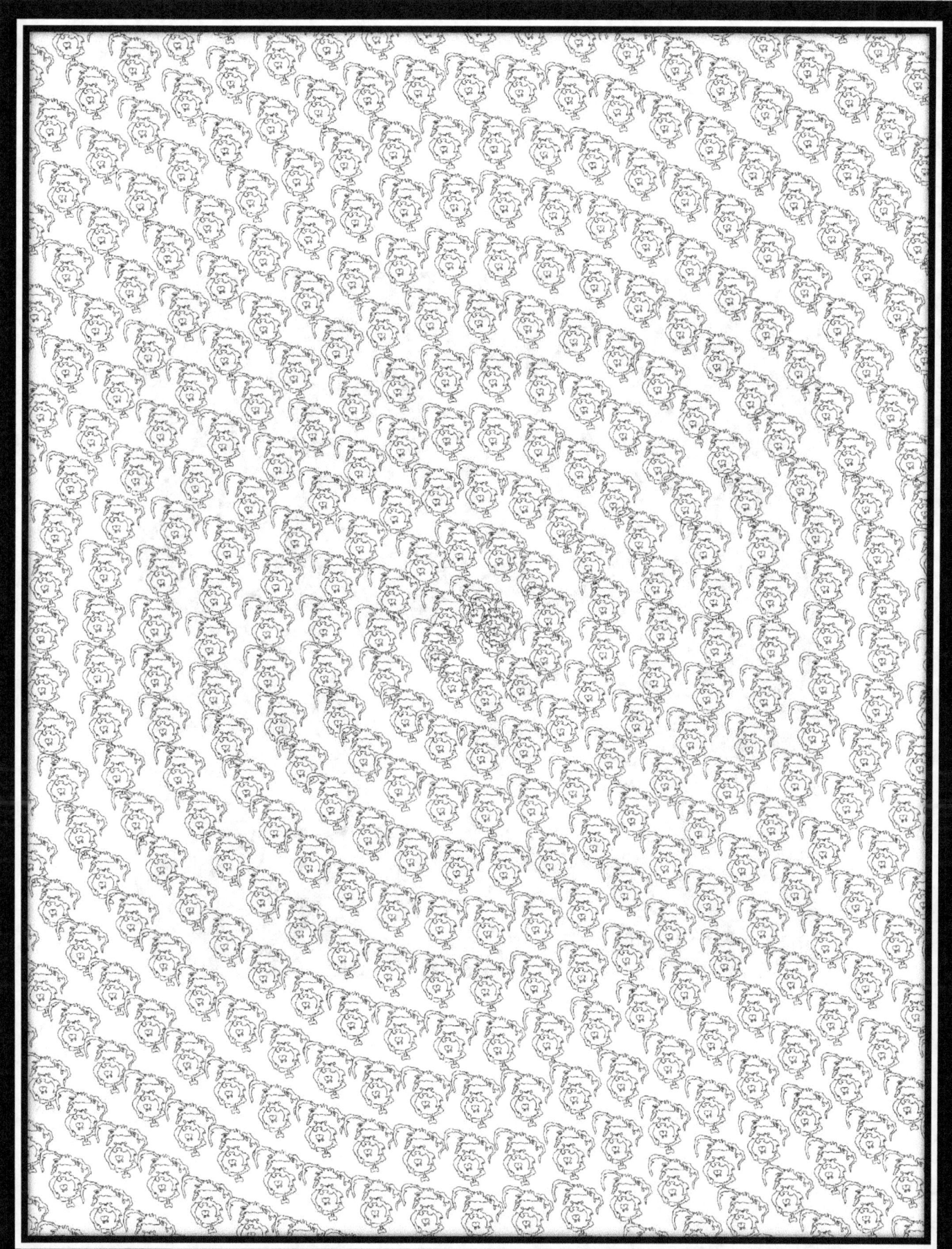

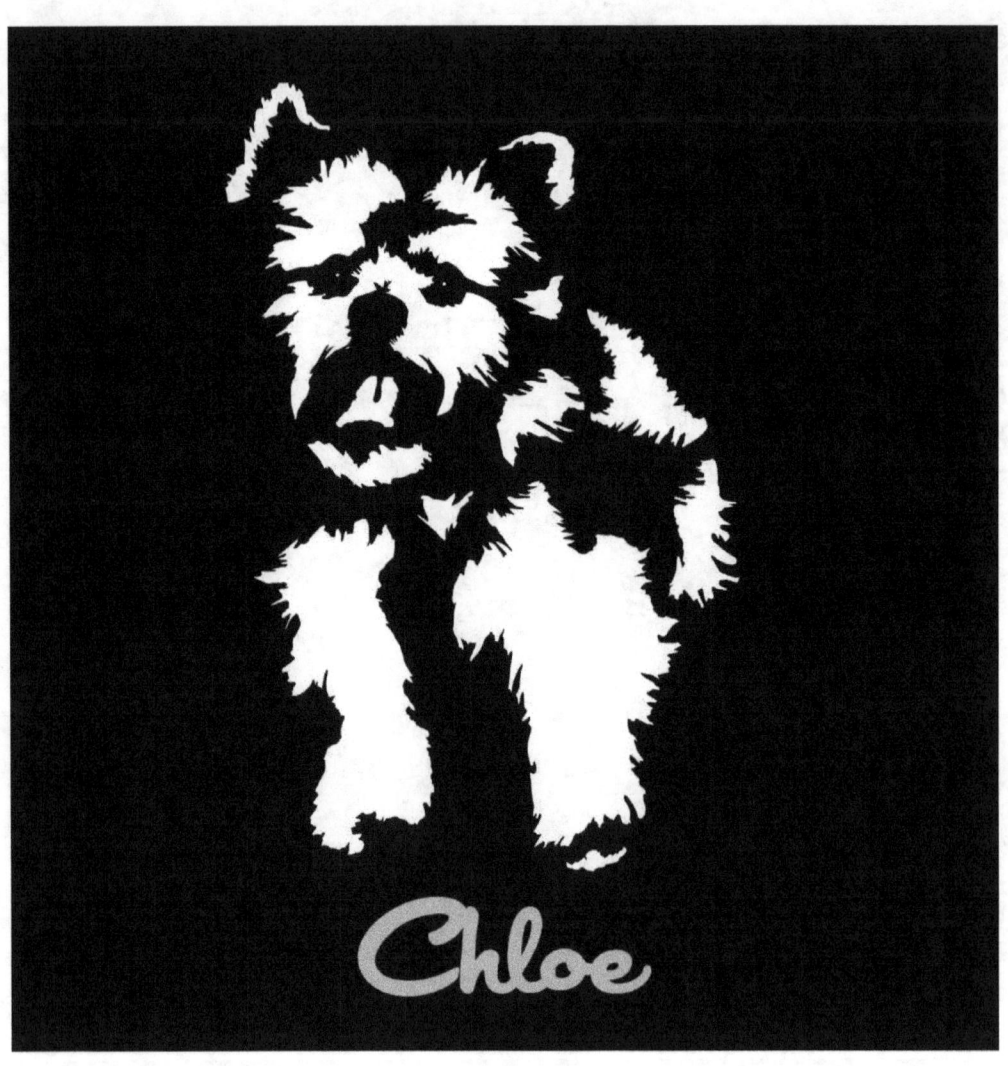

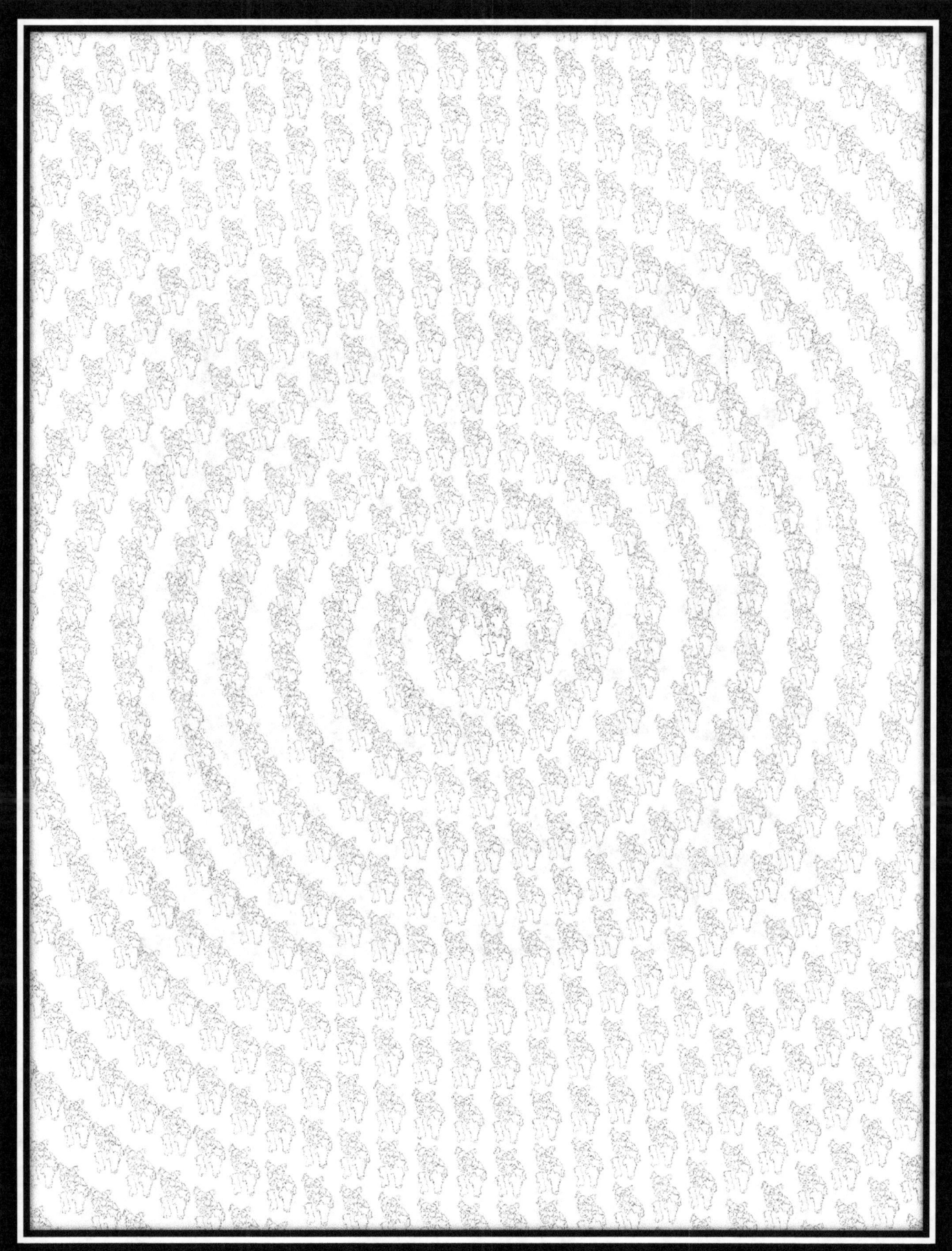

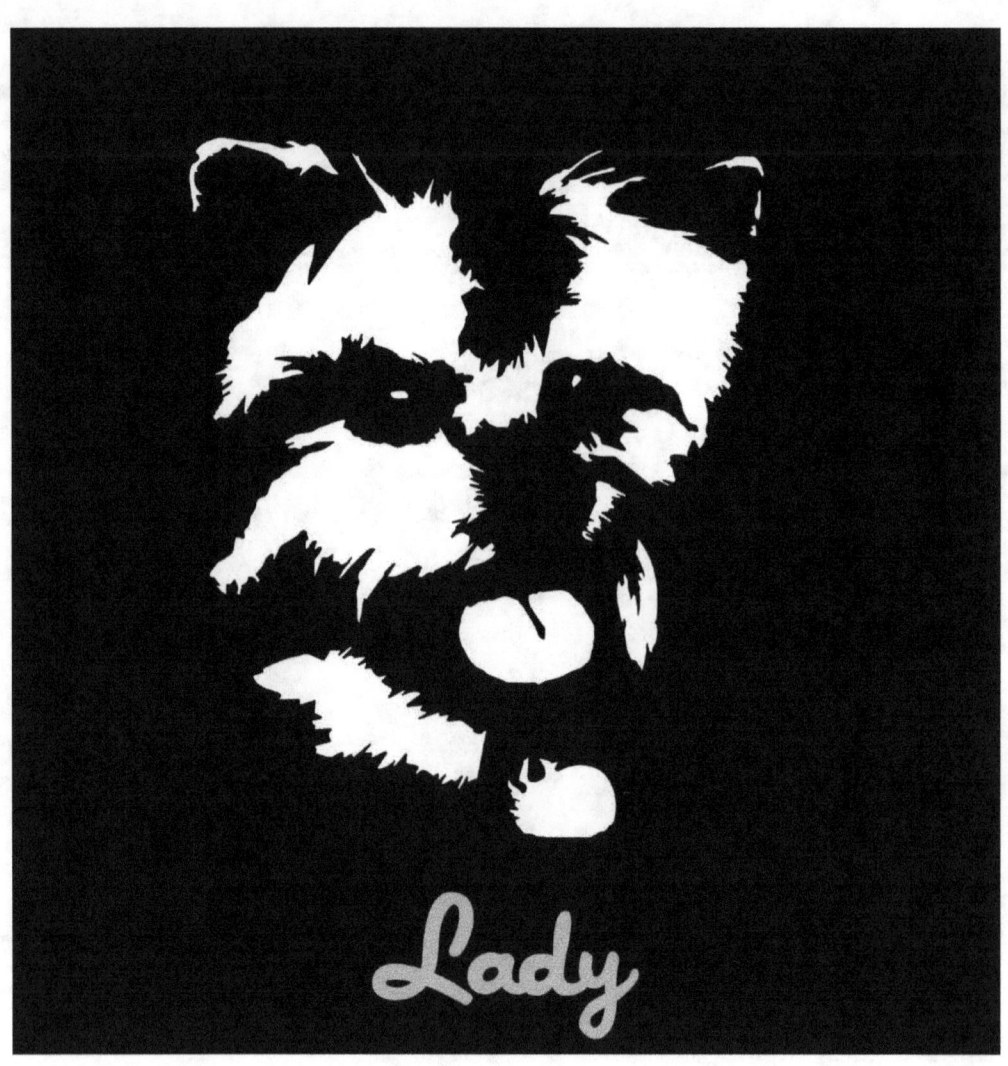

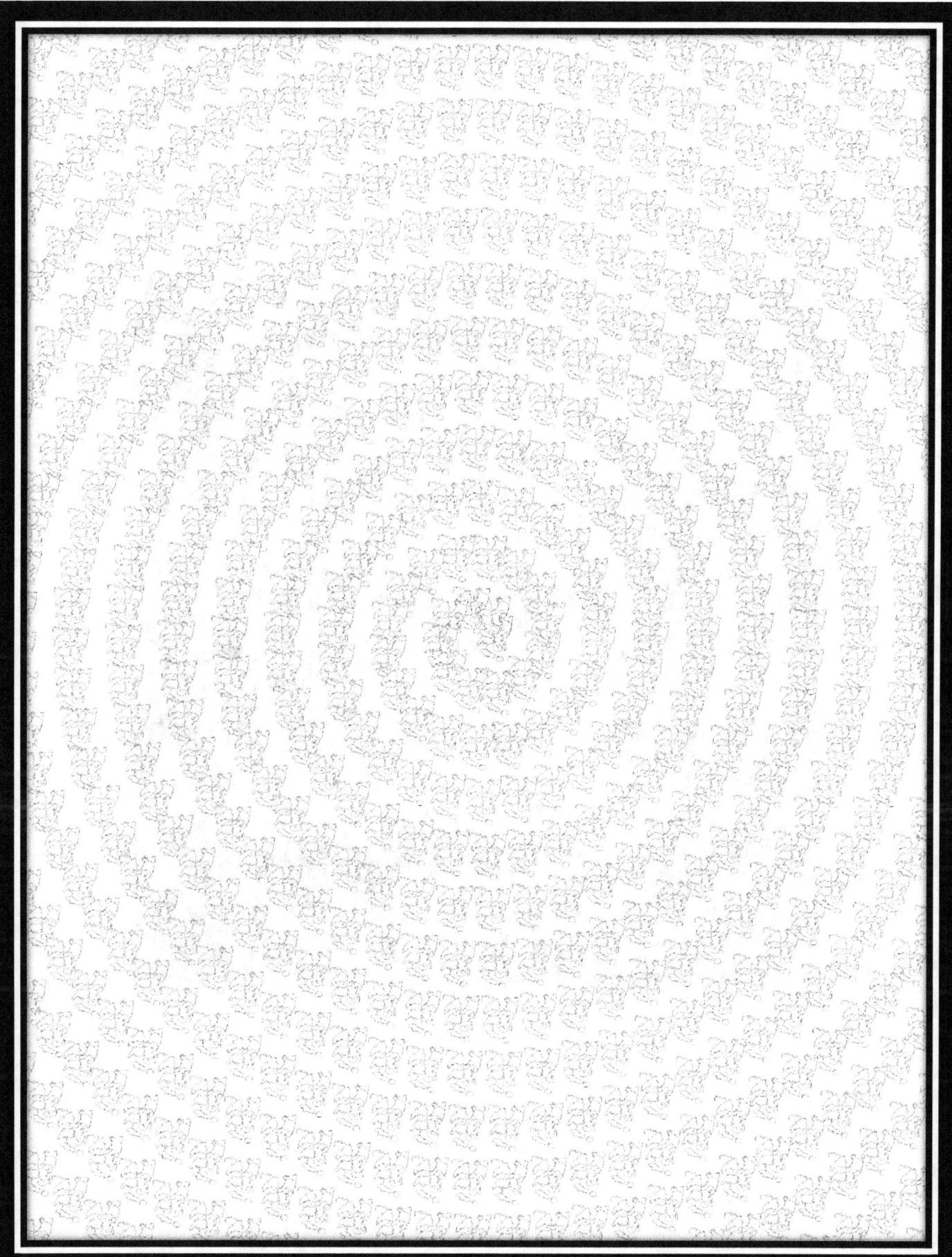

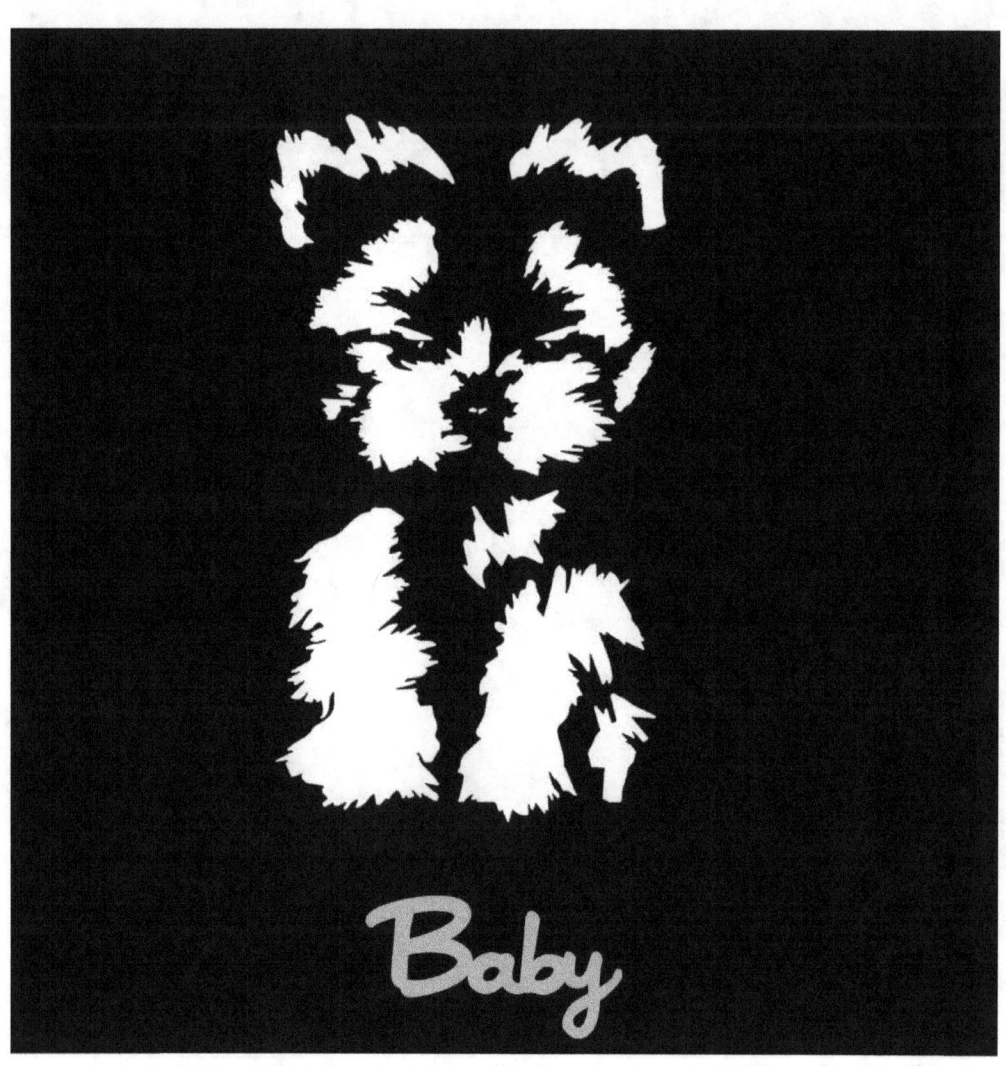

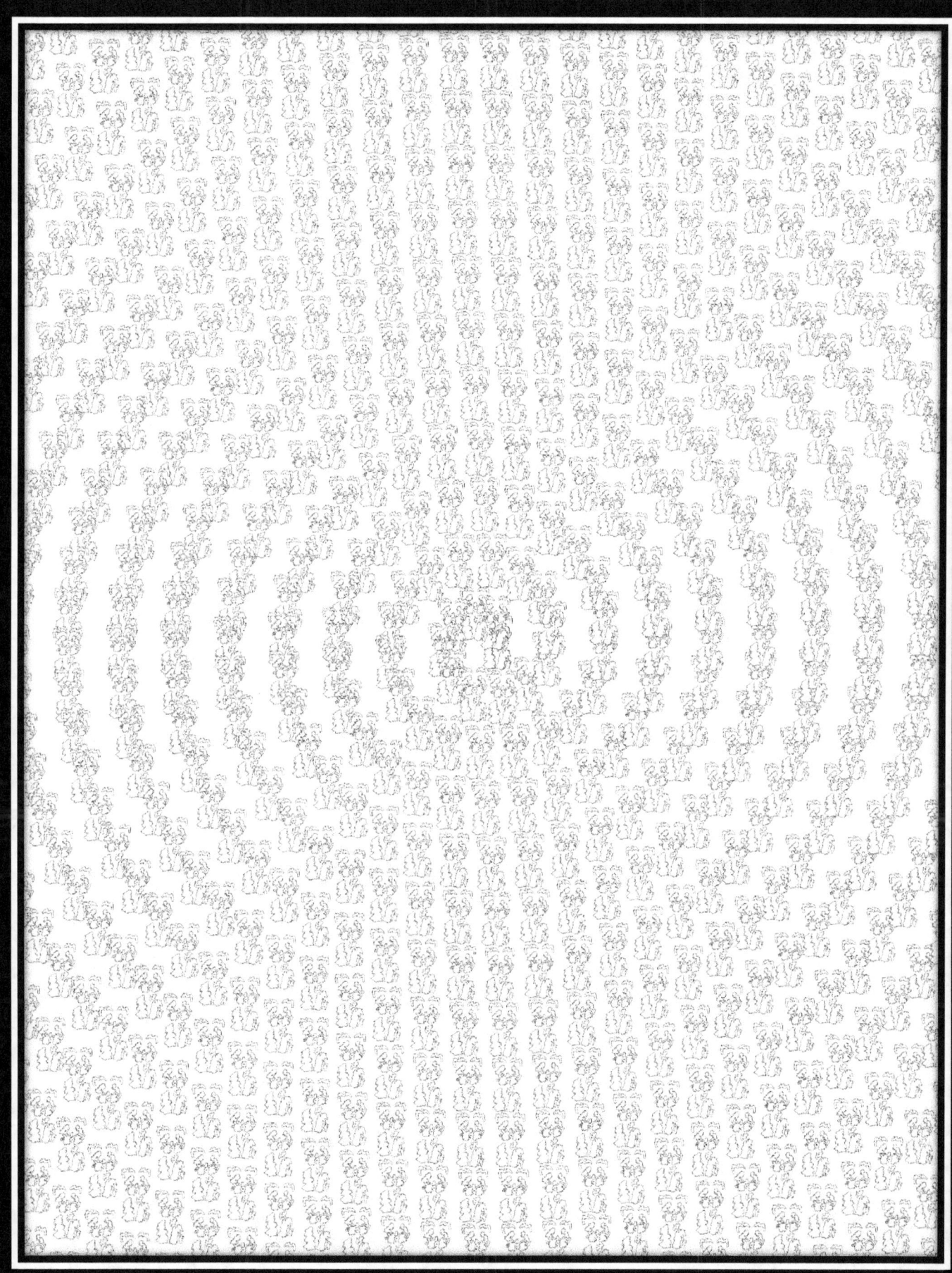

ROTATION PATTERNS

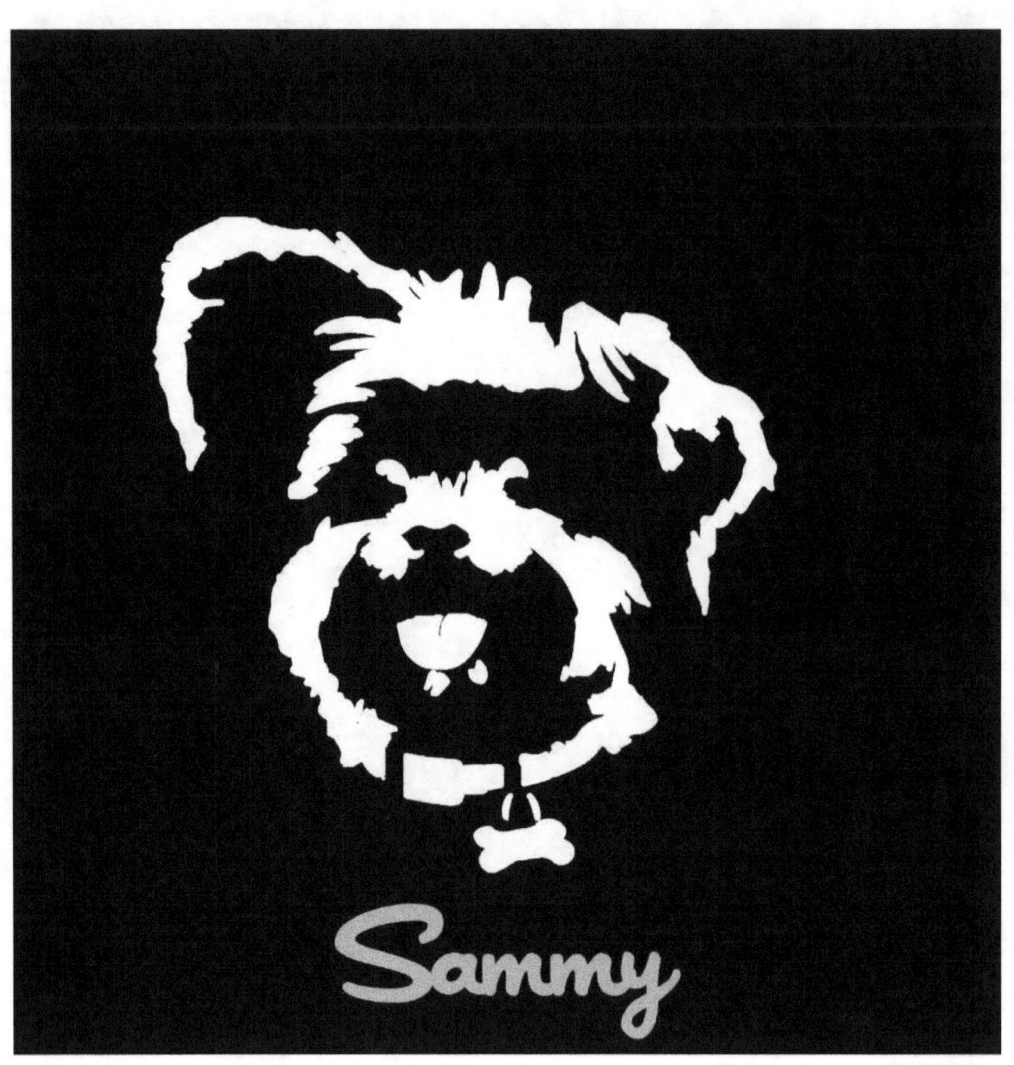

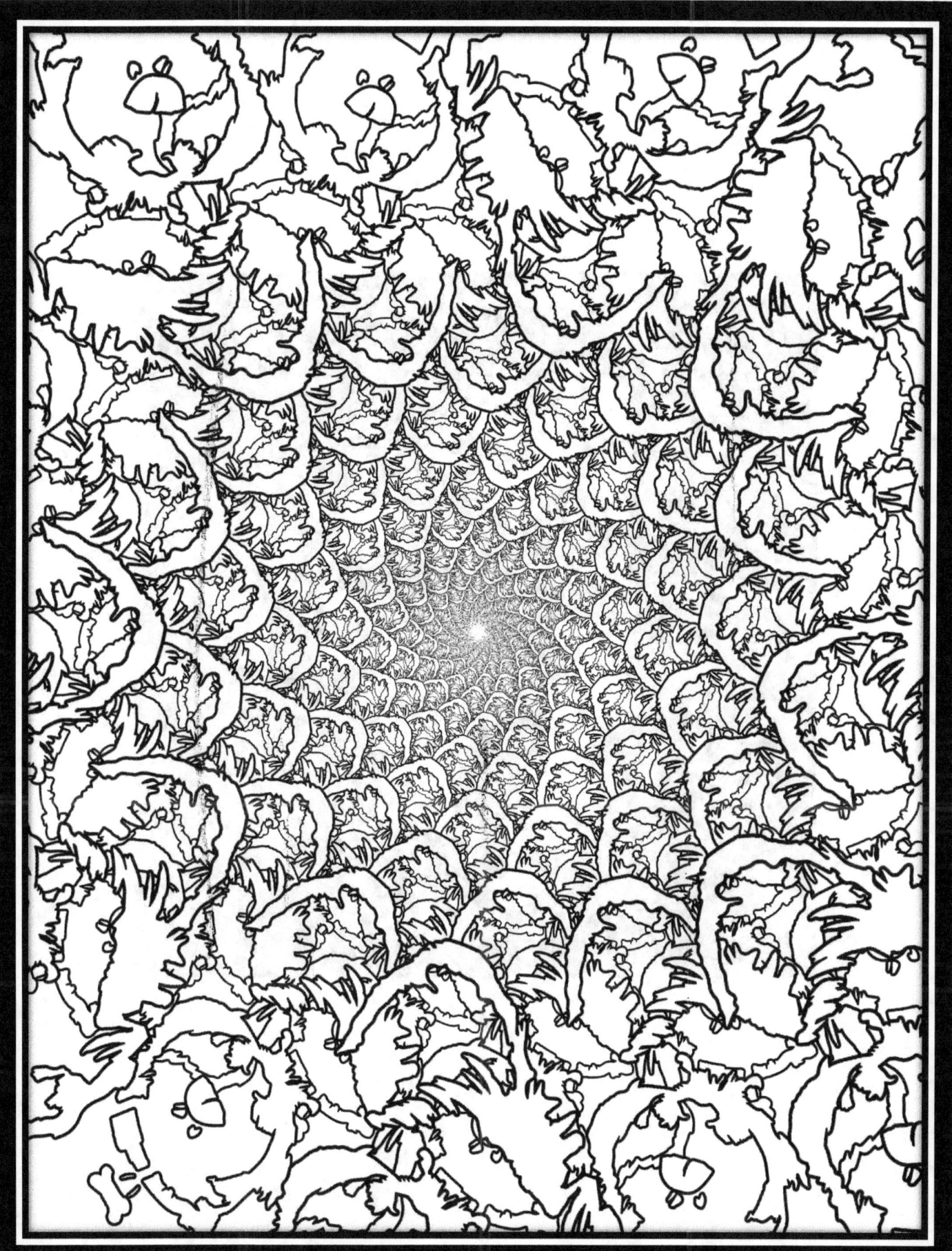

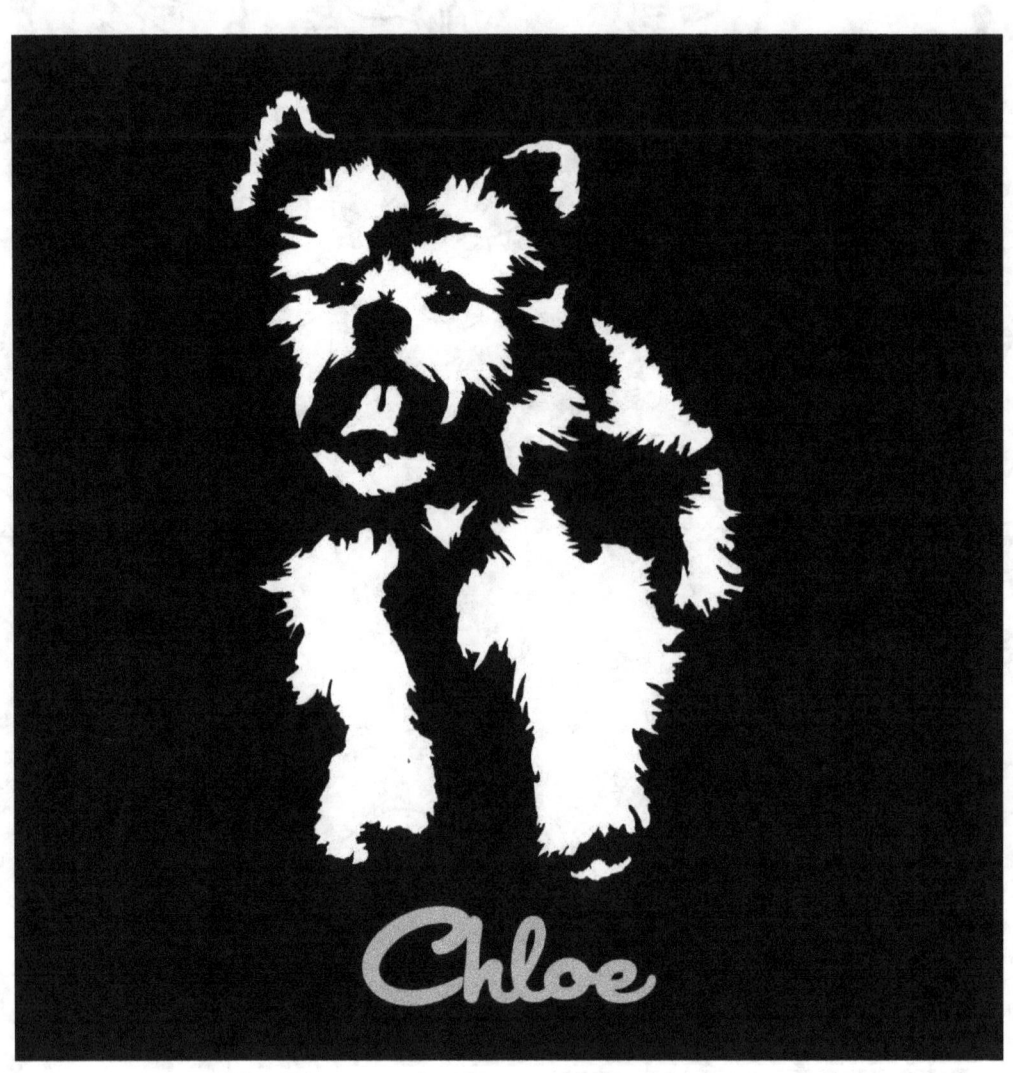

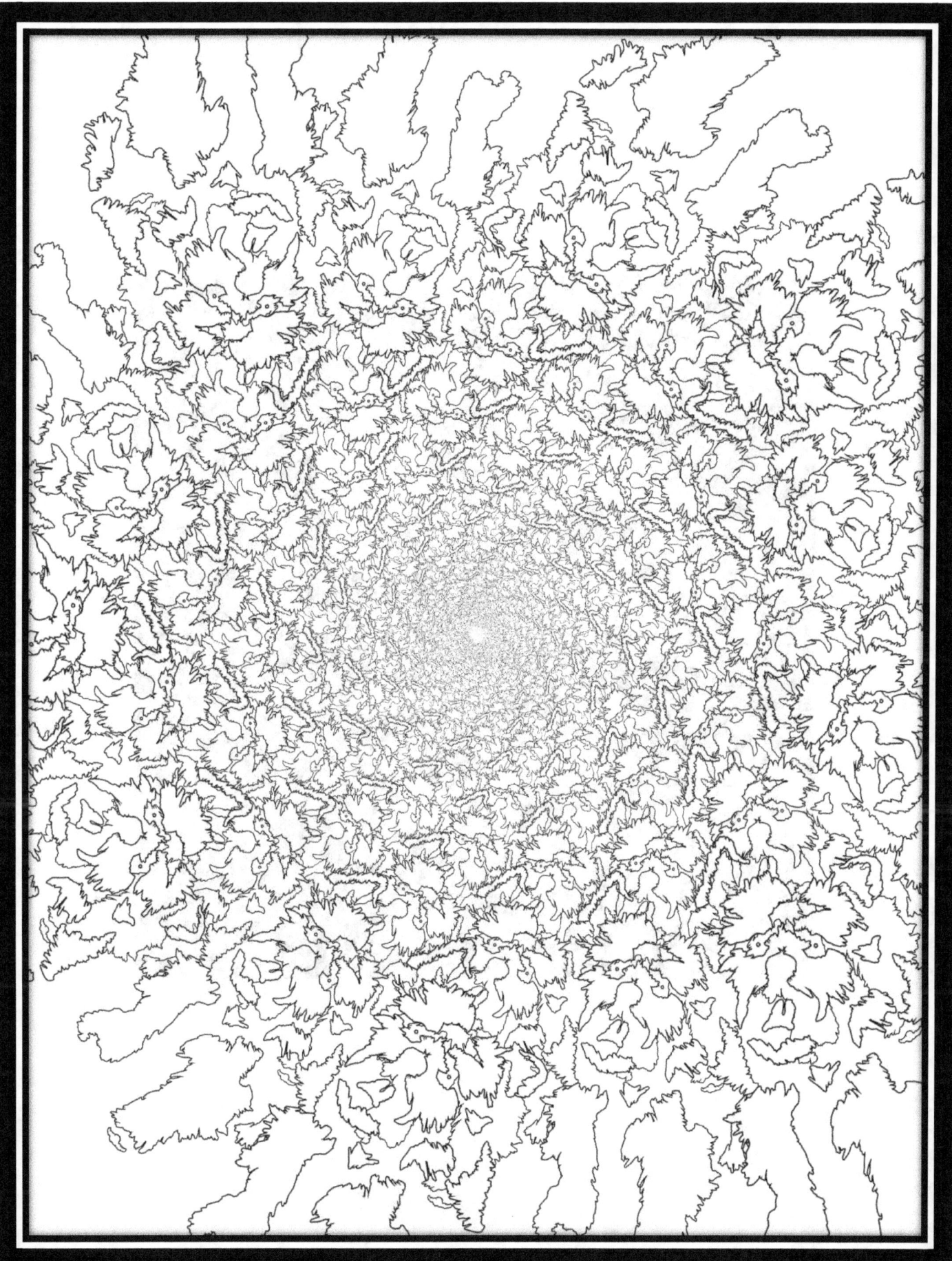

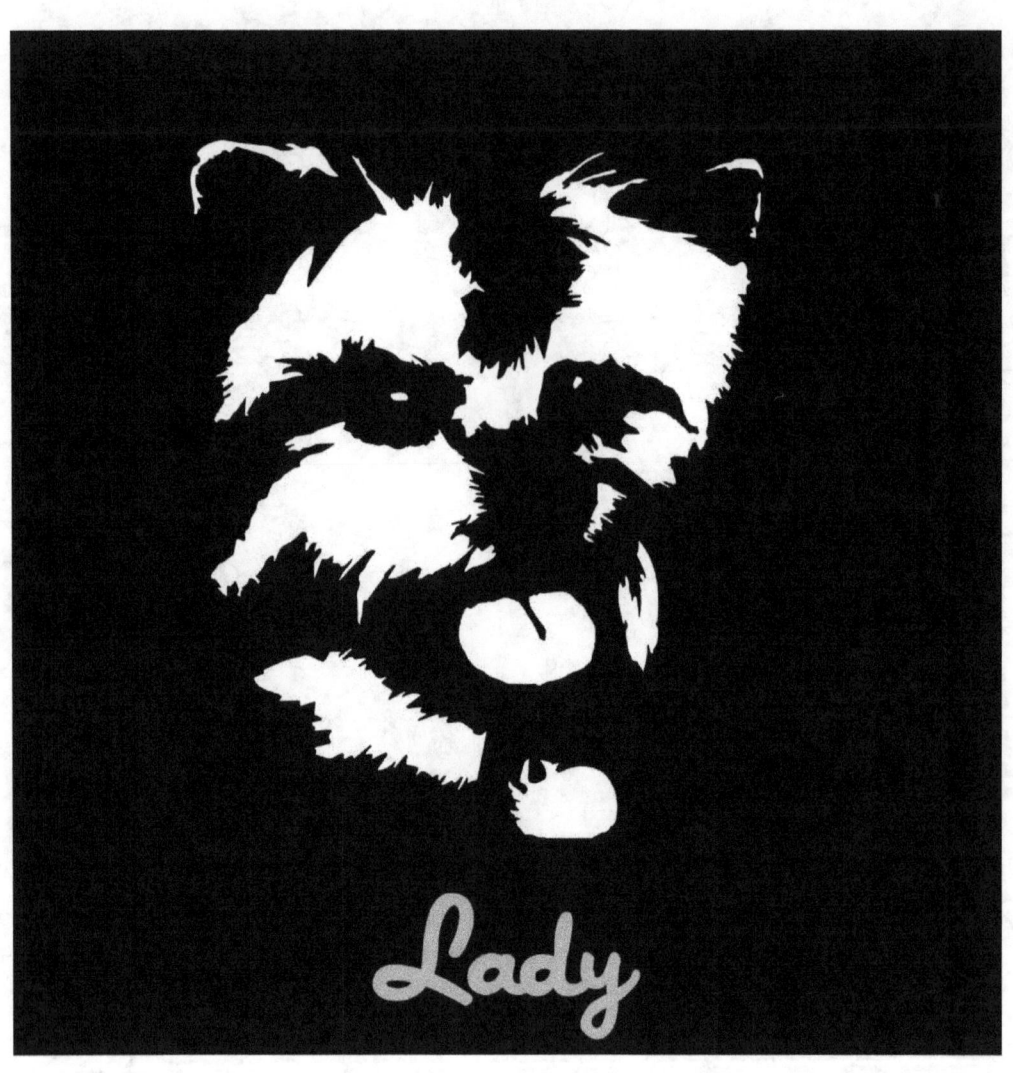

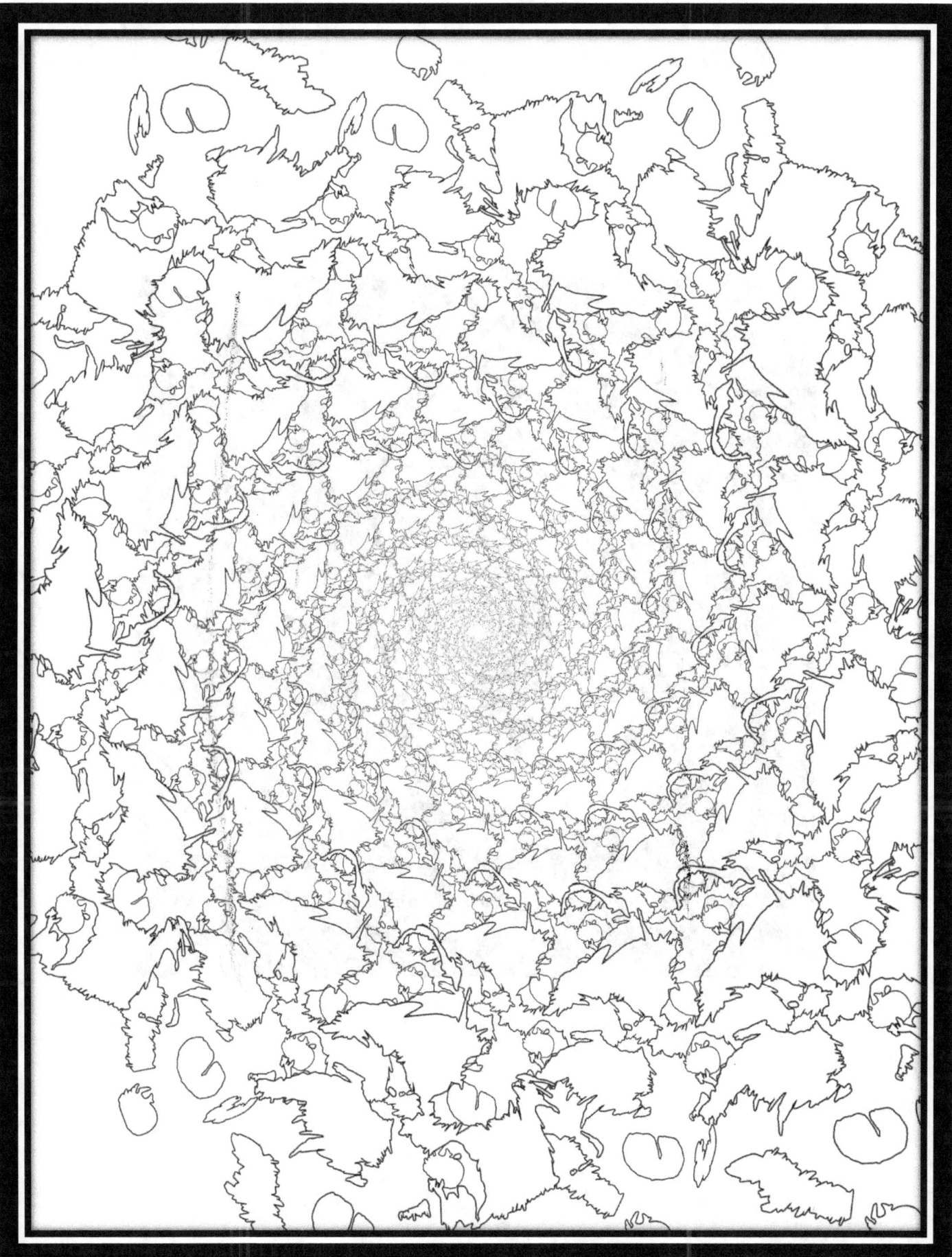

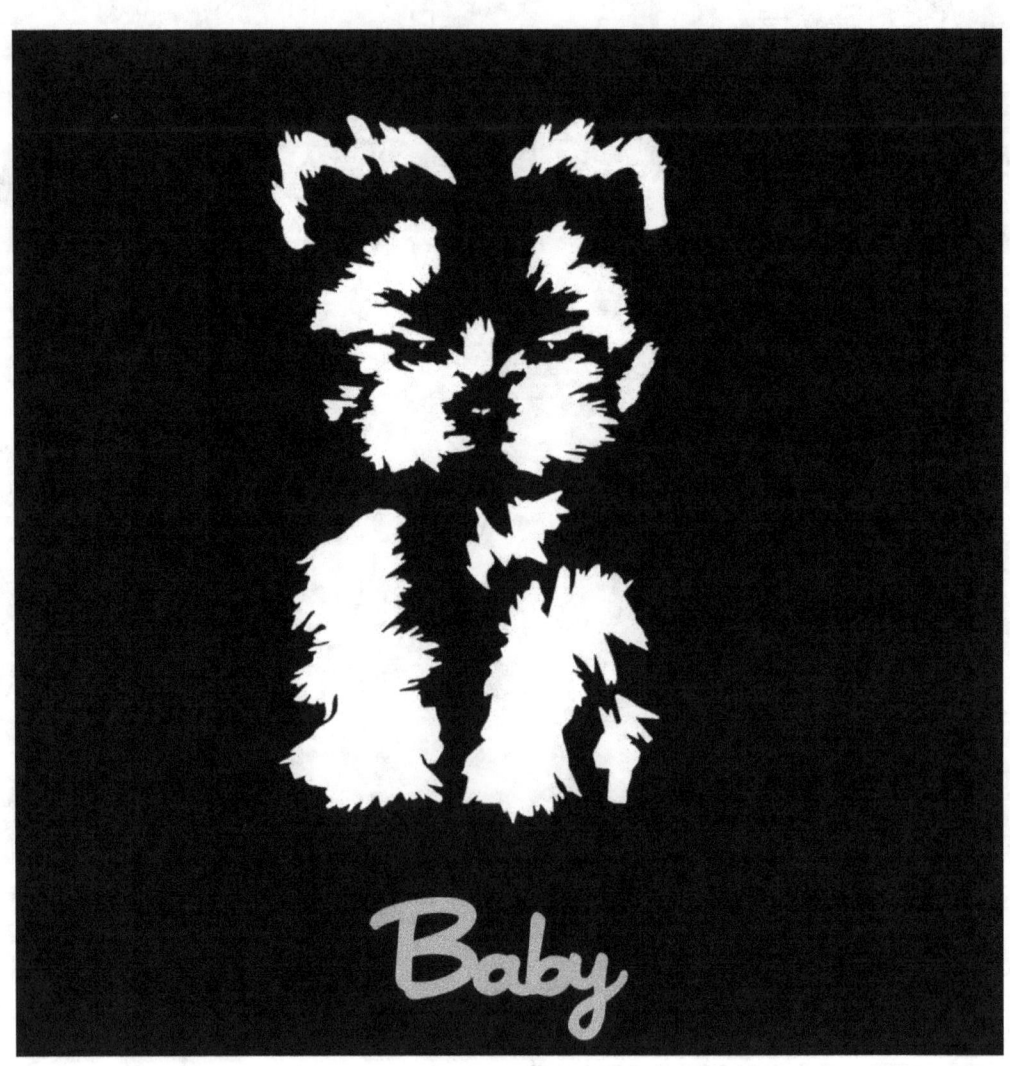

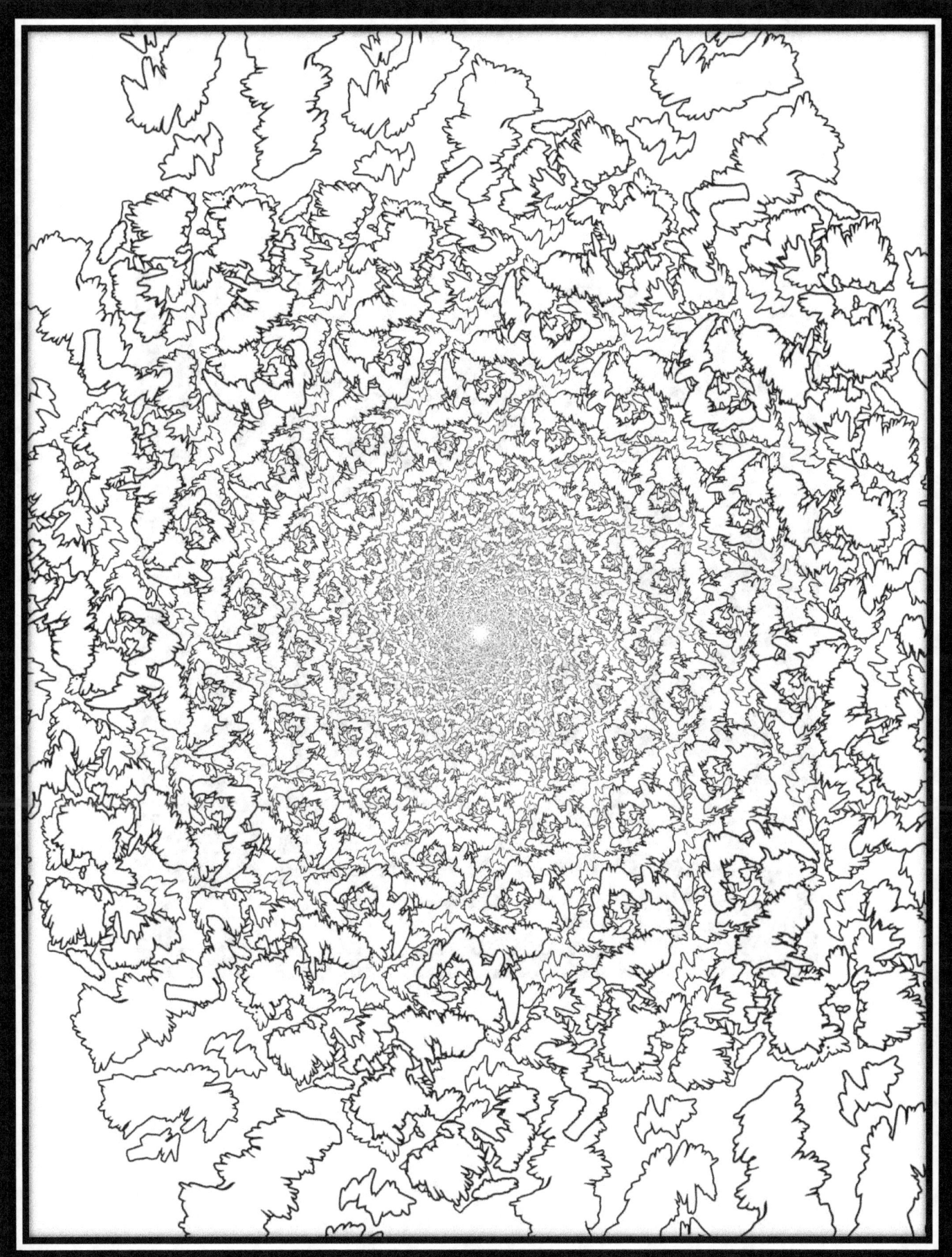

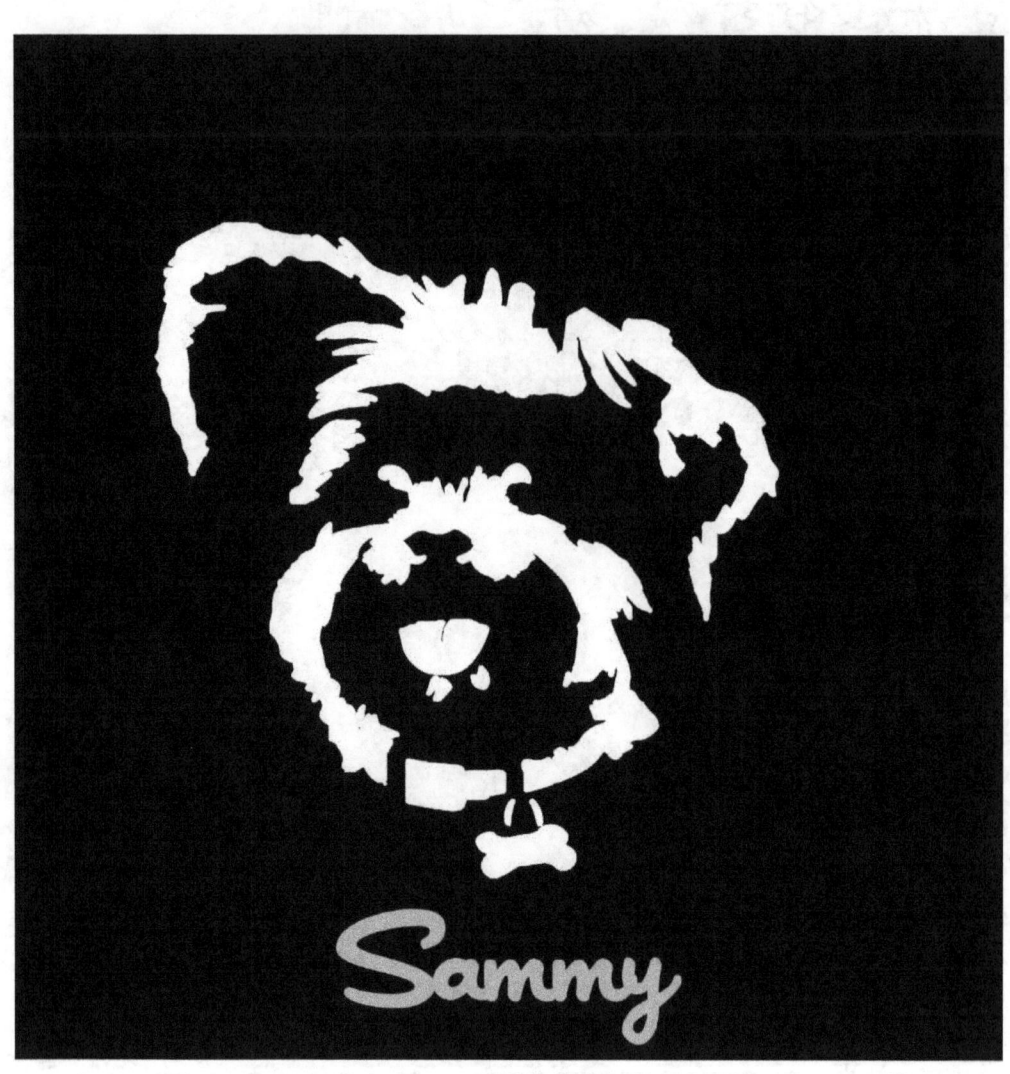

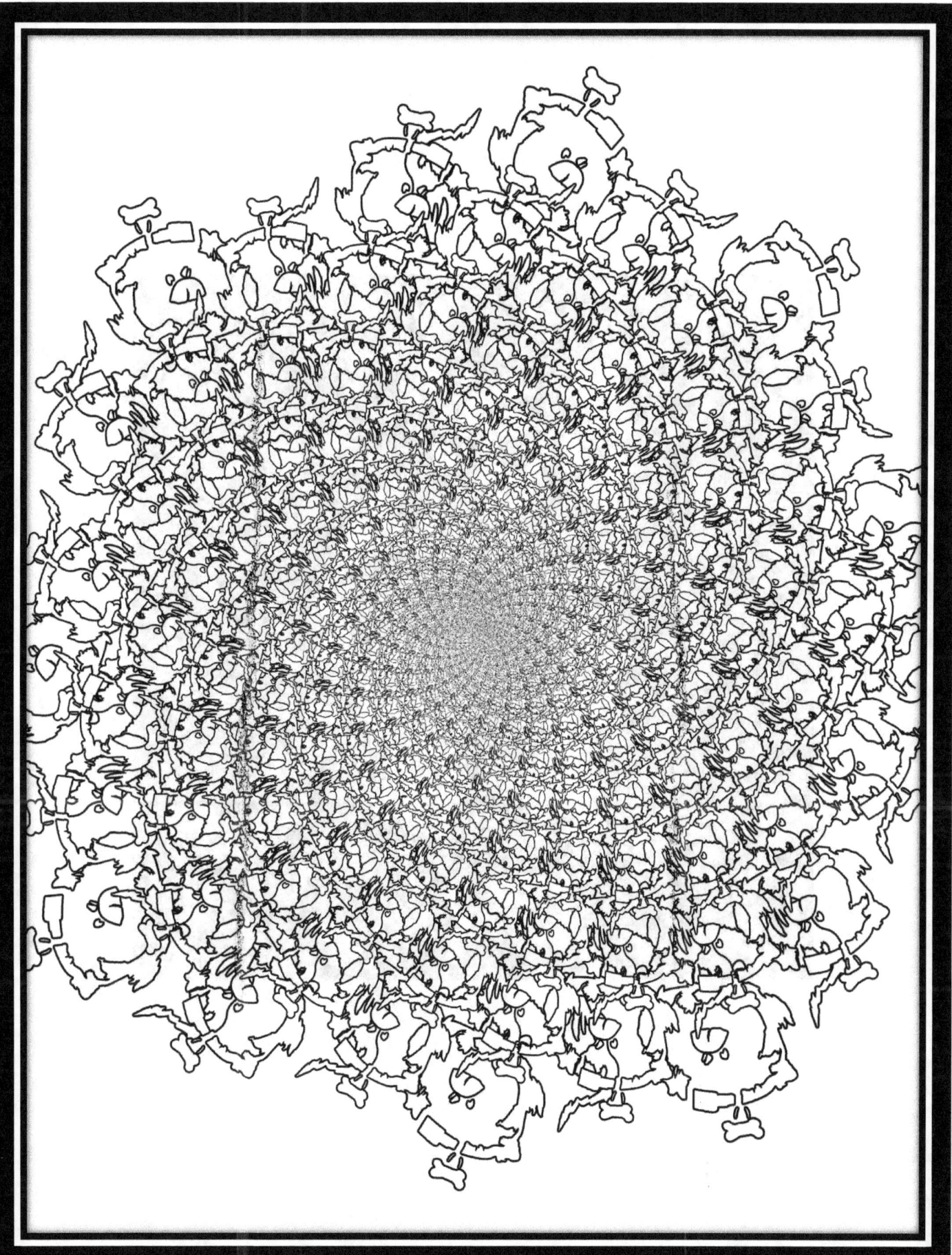

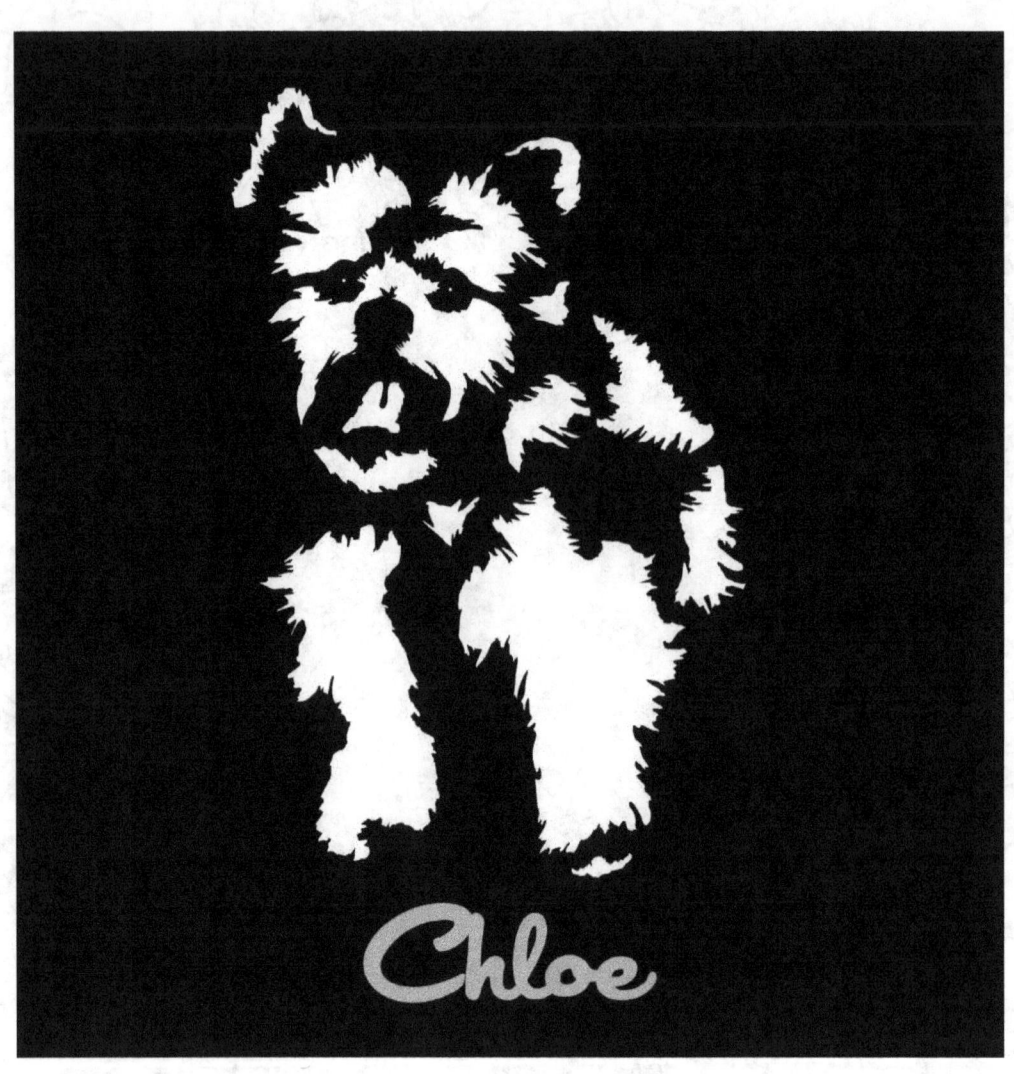

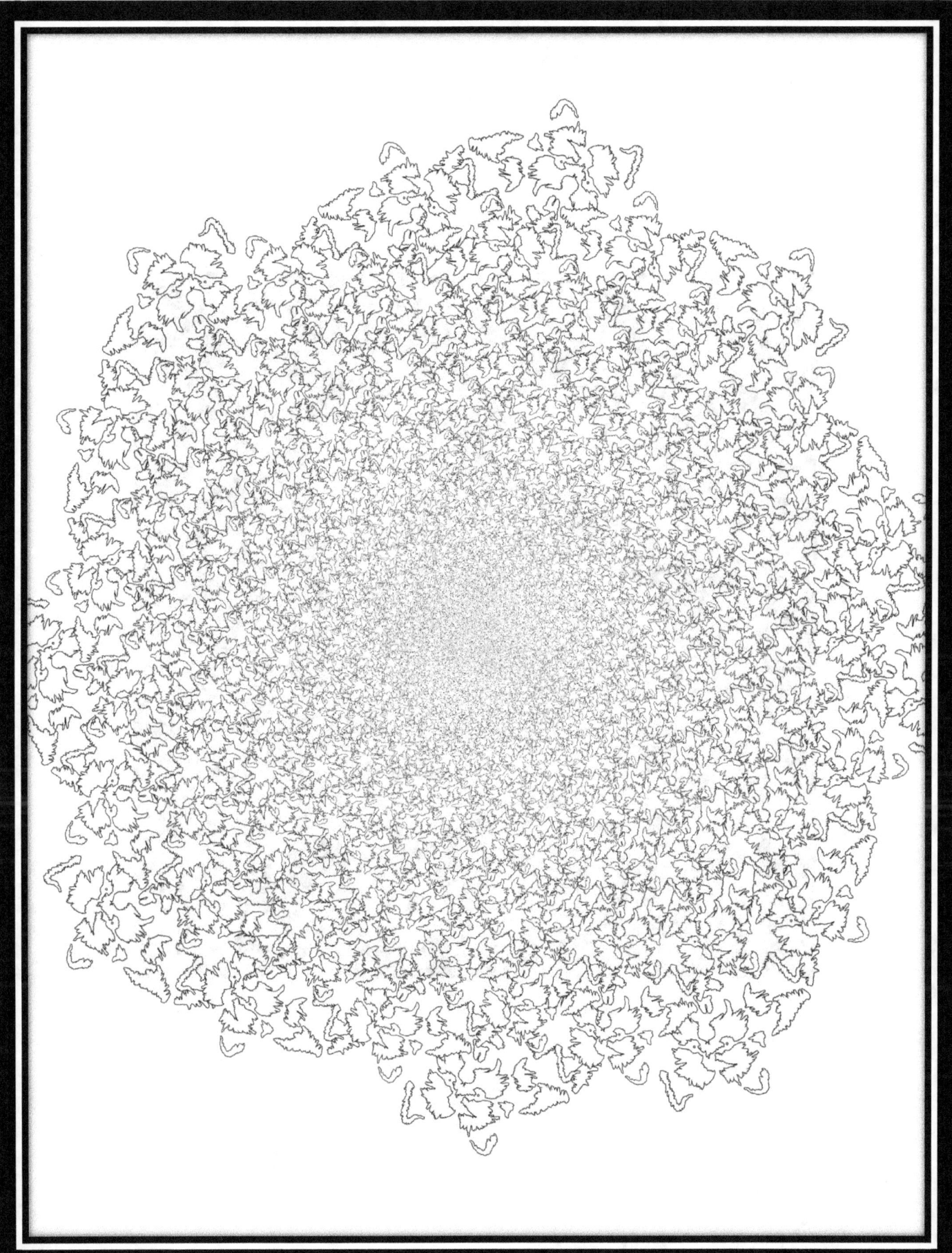

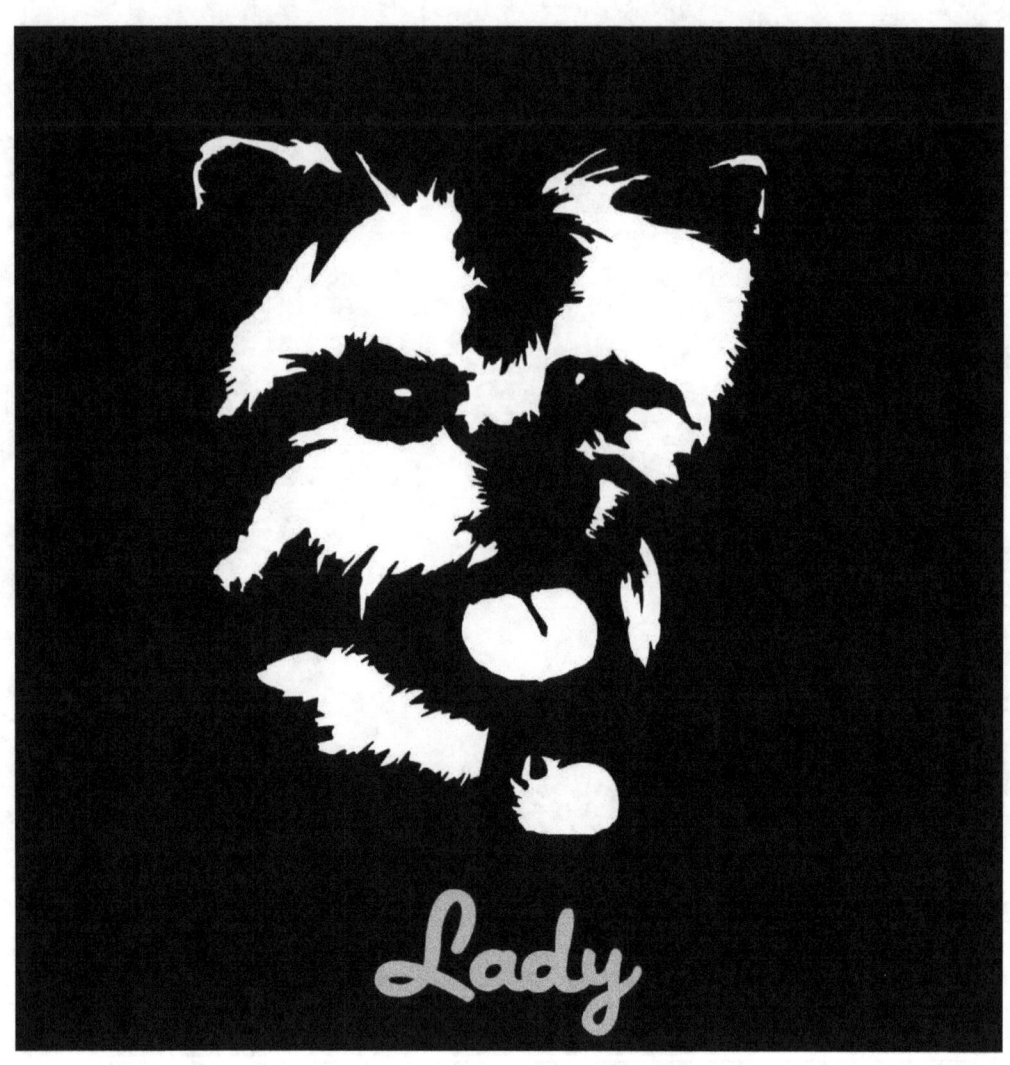

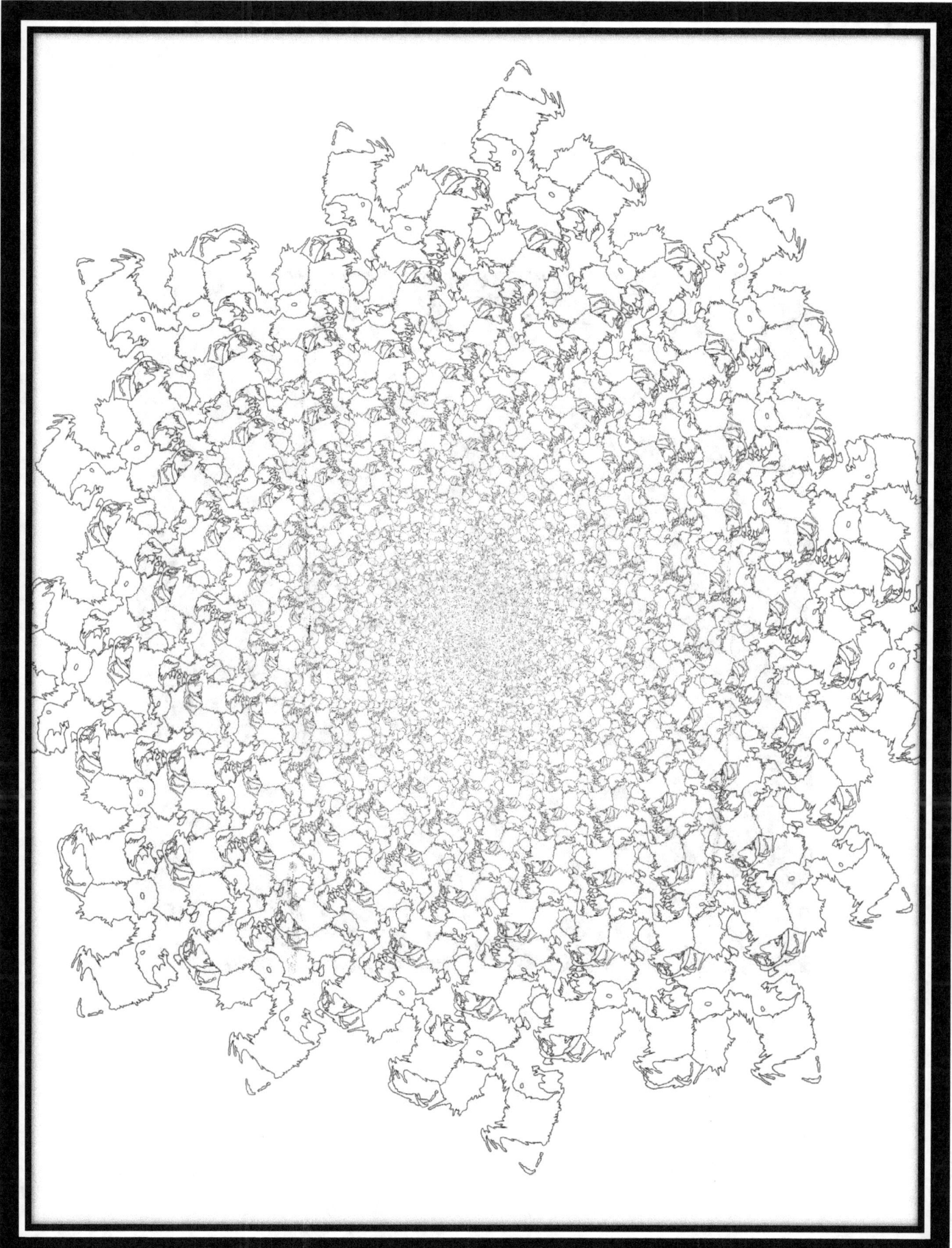

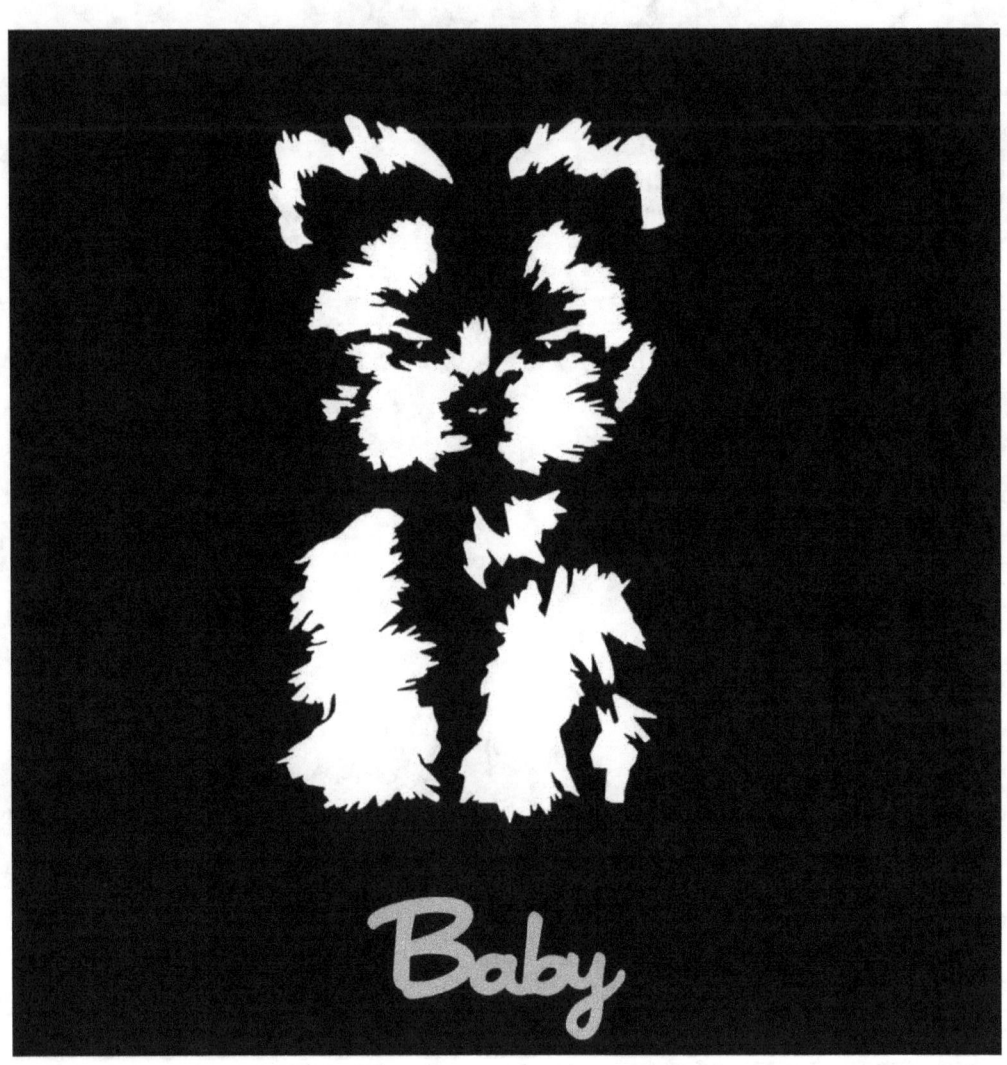

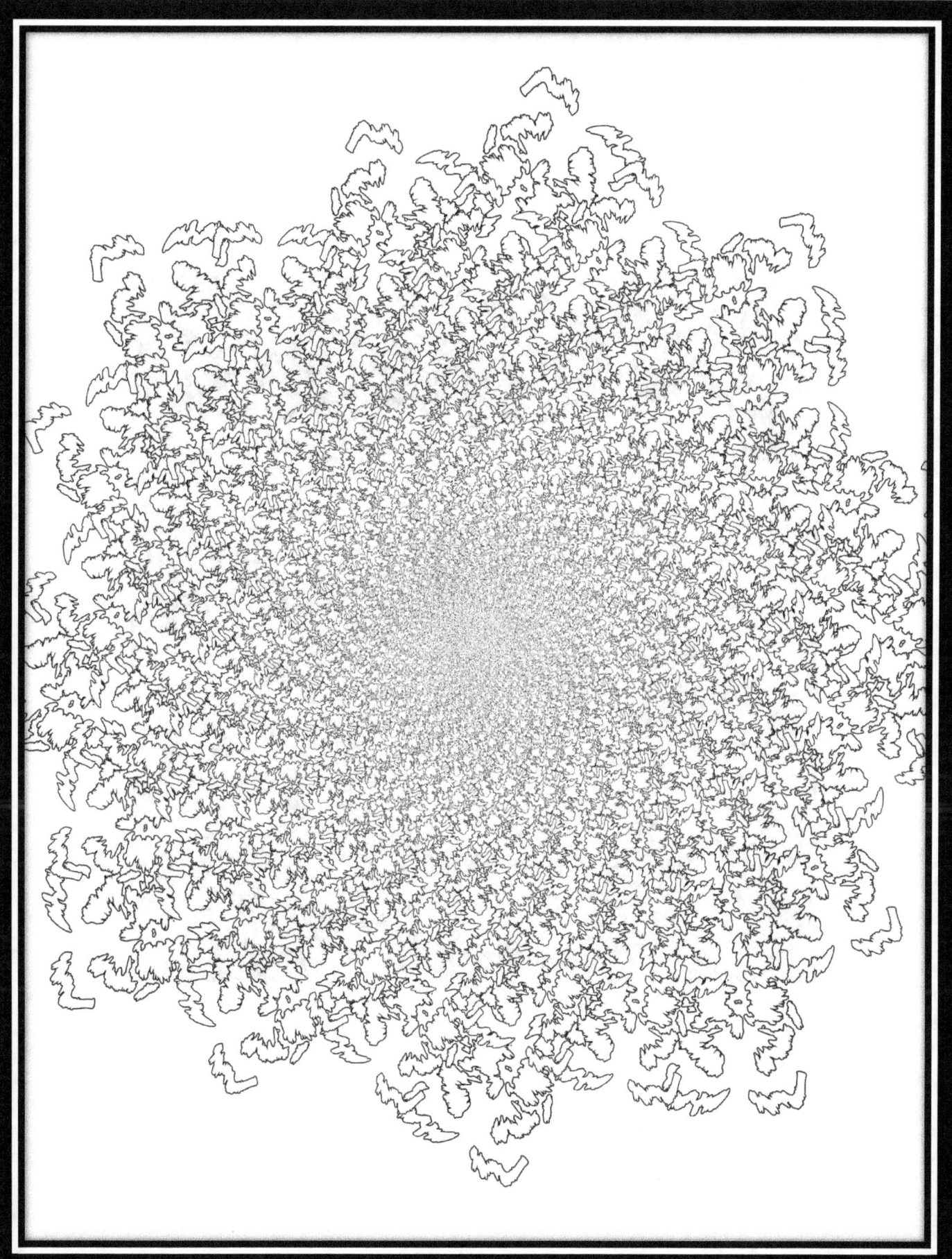

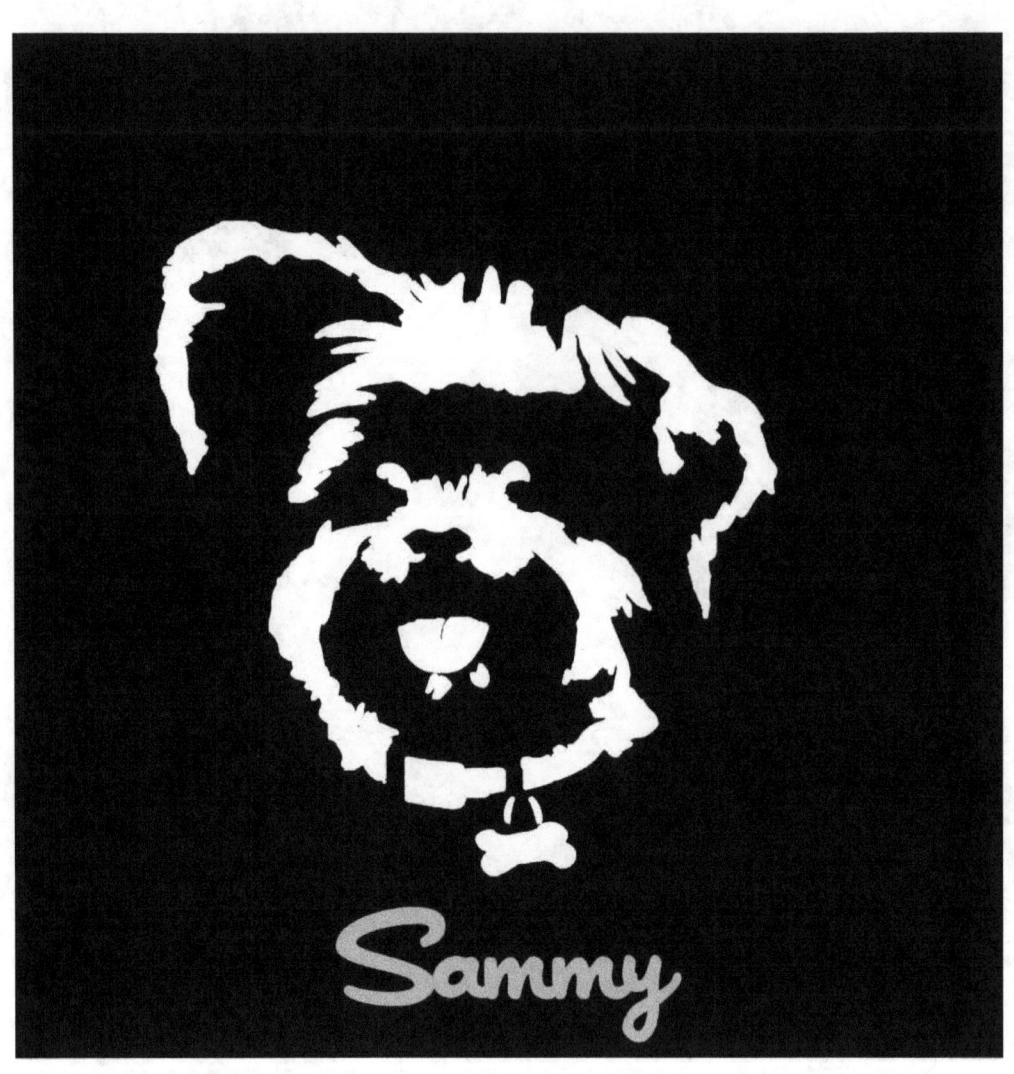

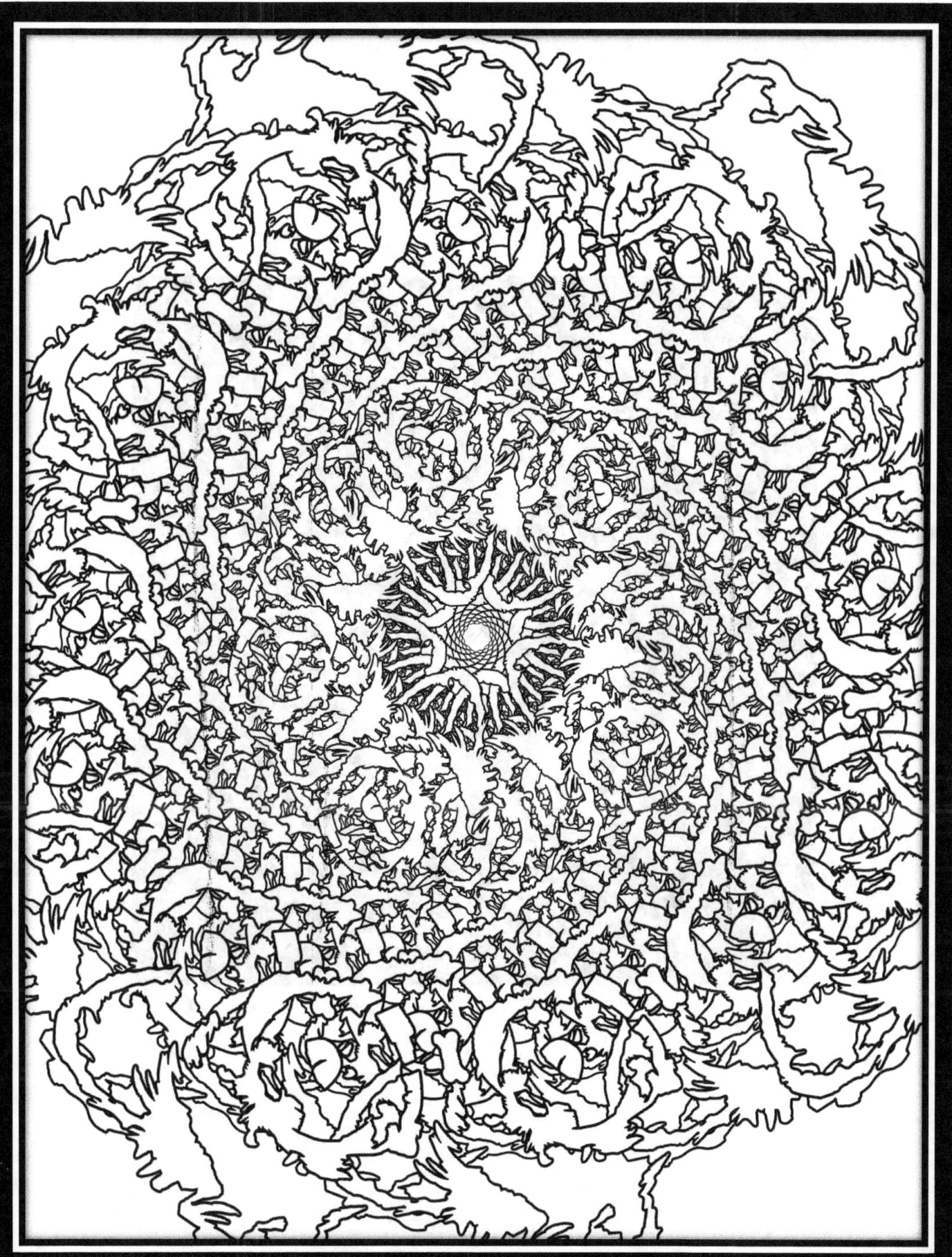

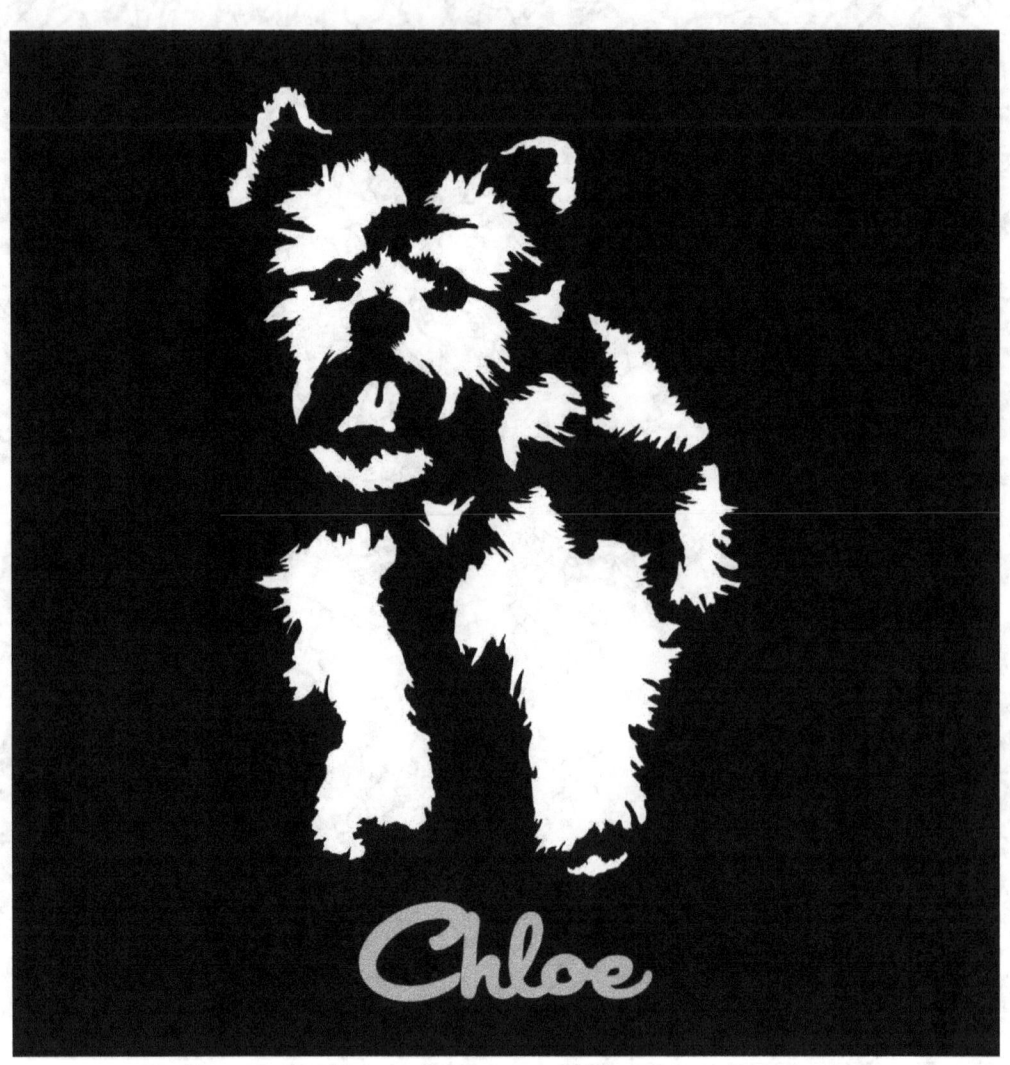

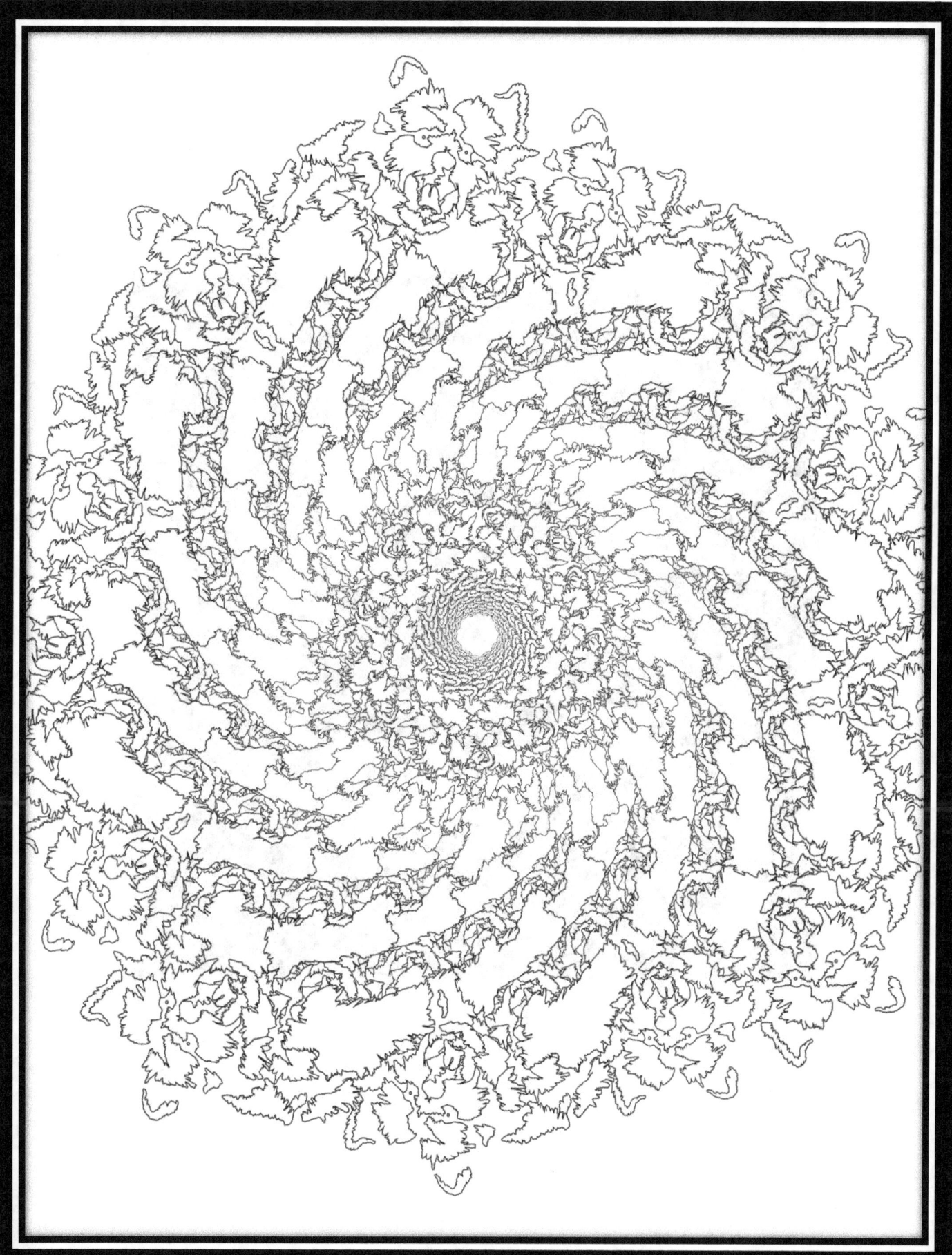

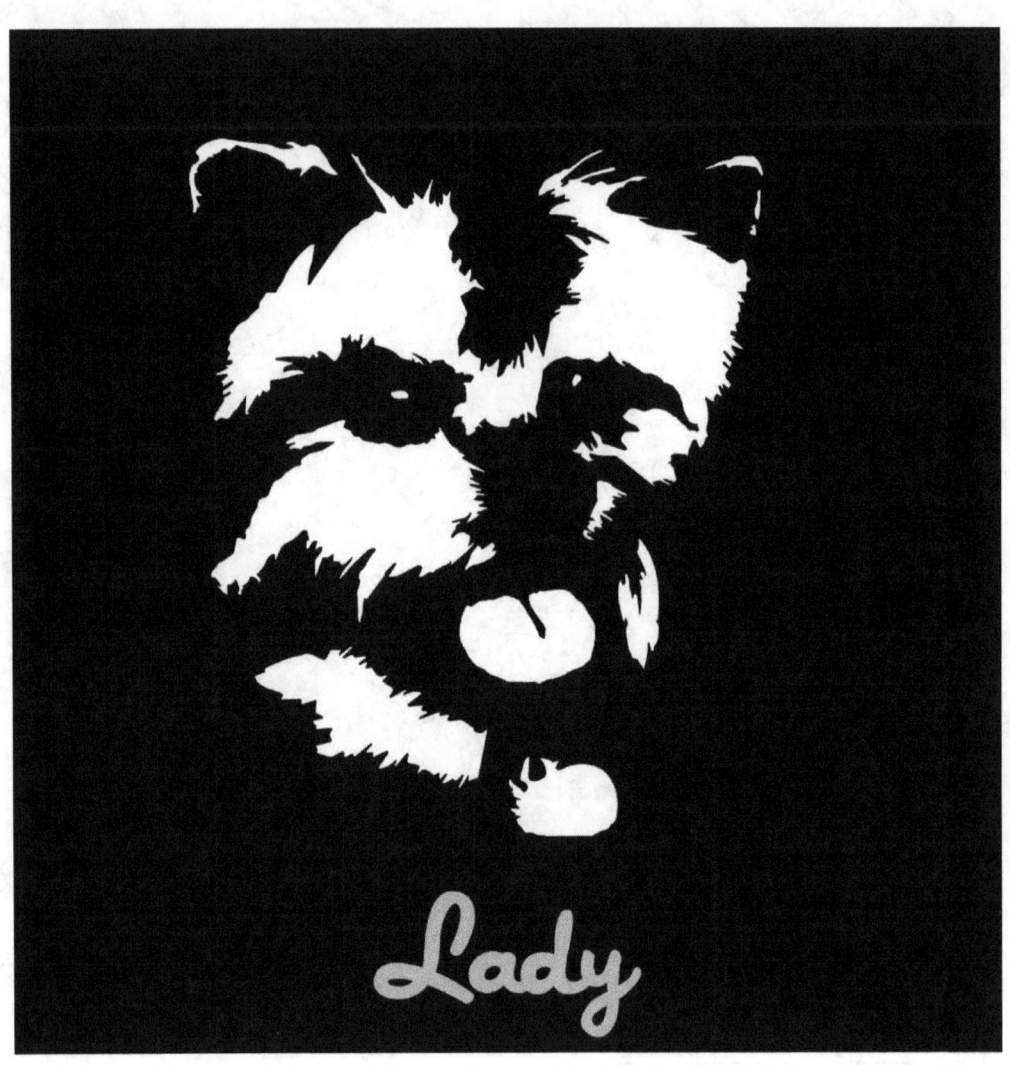

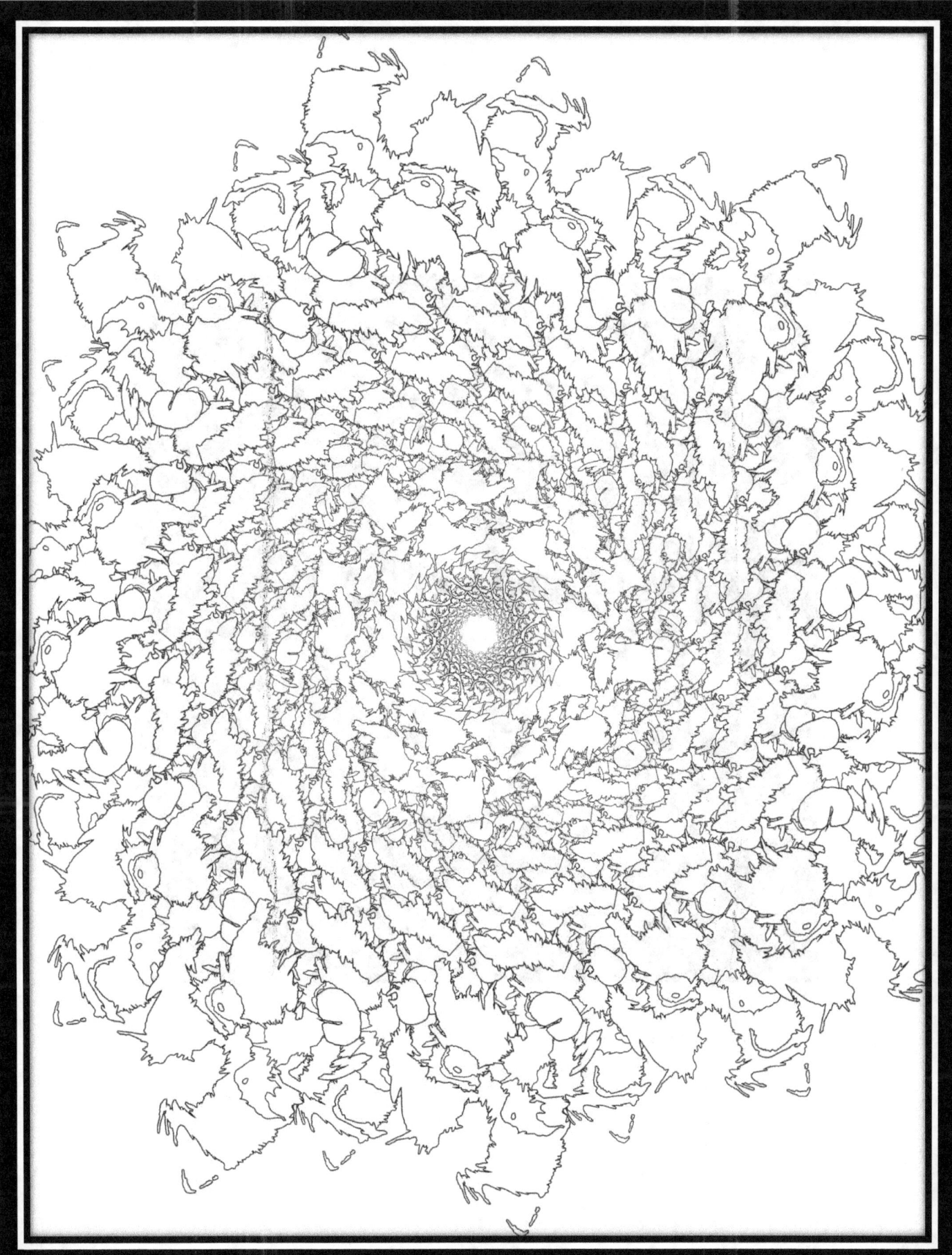

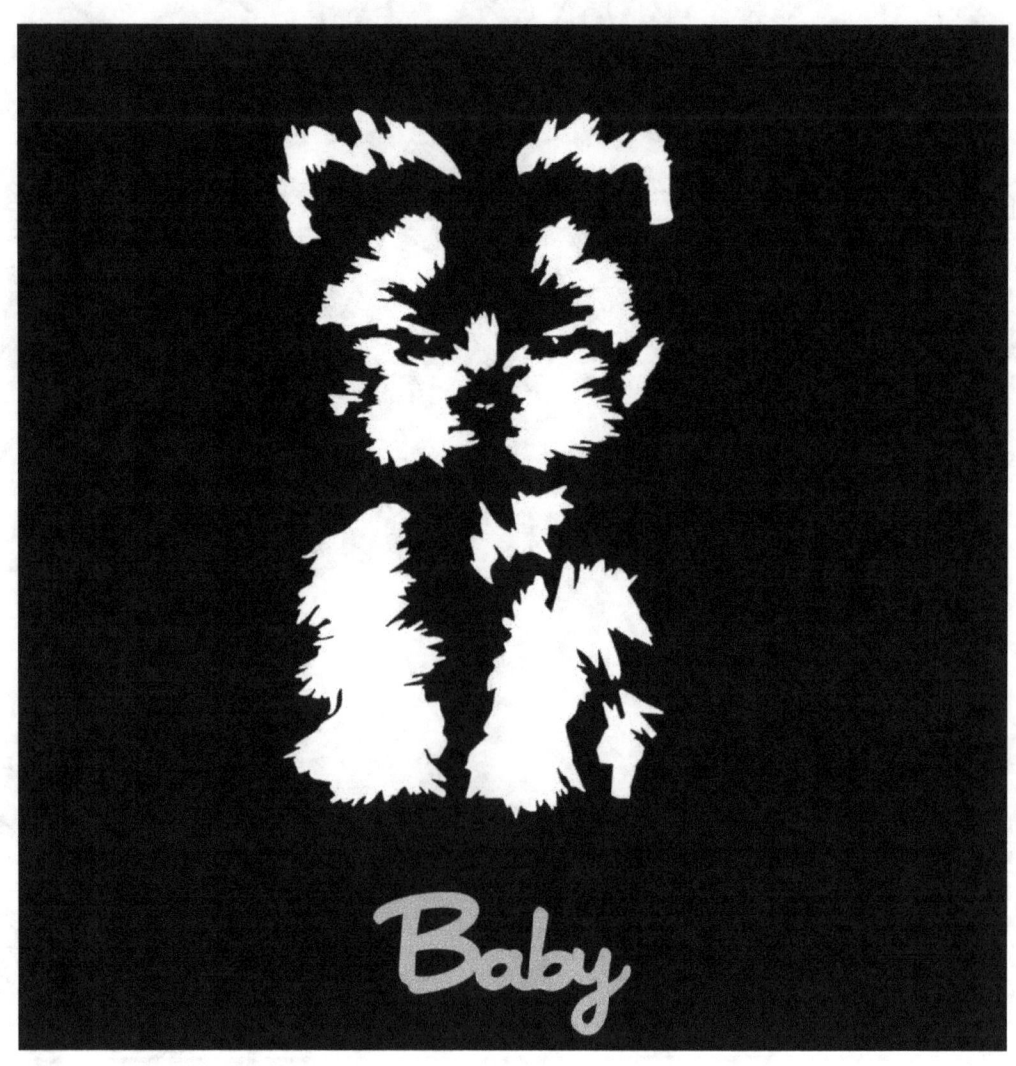

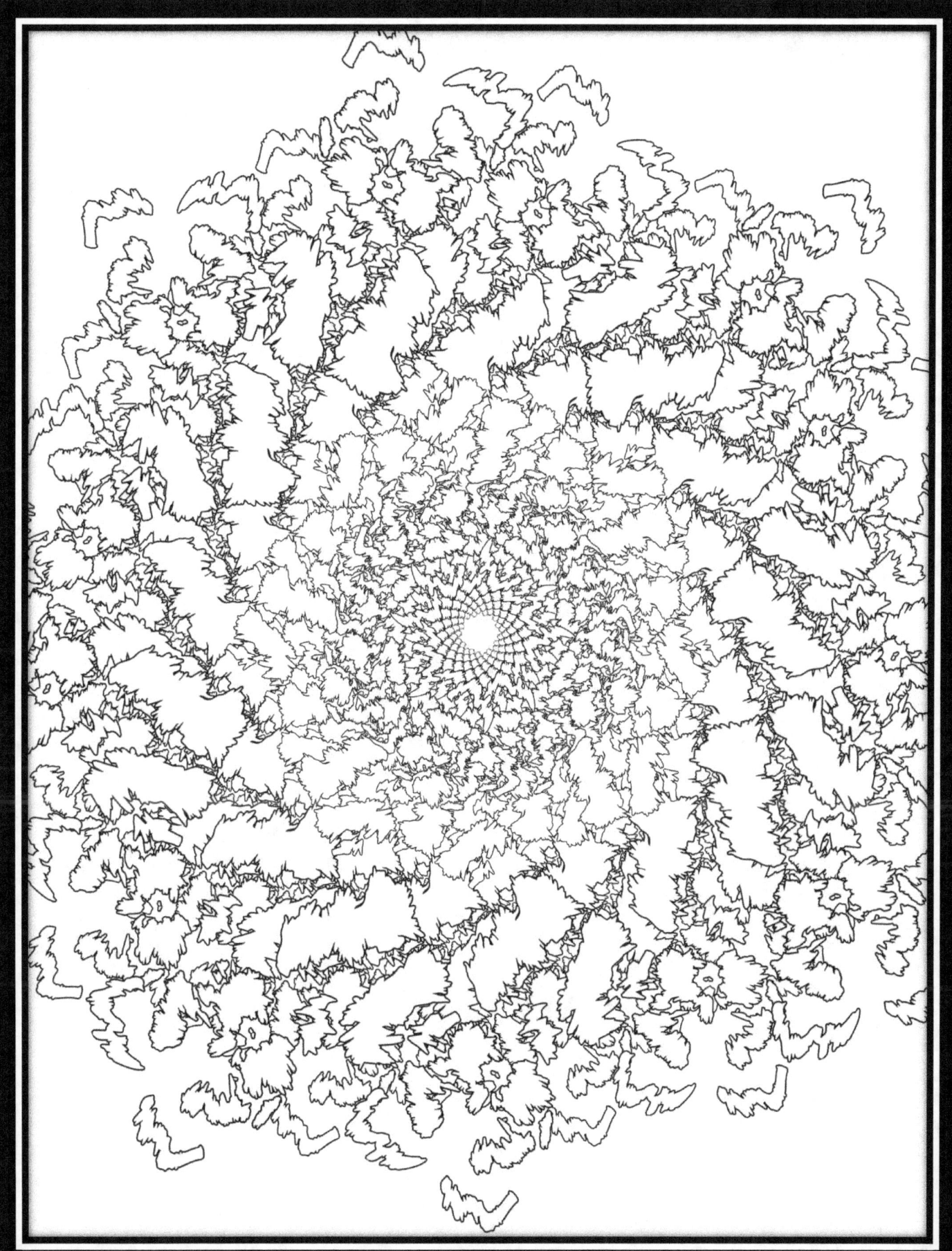

WALLPAPER PATTERNS

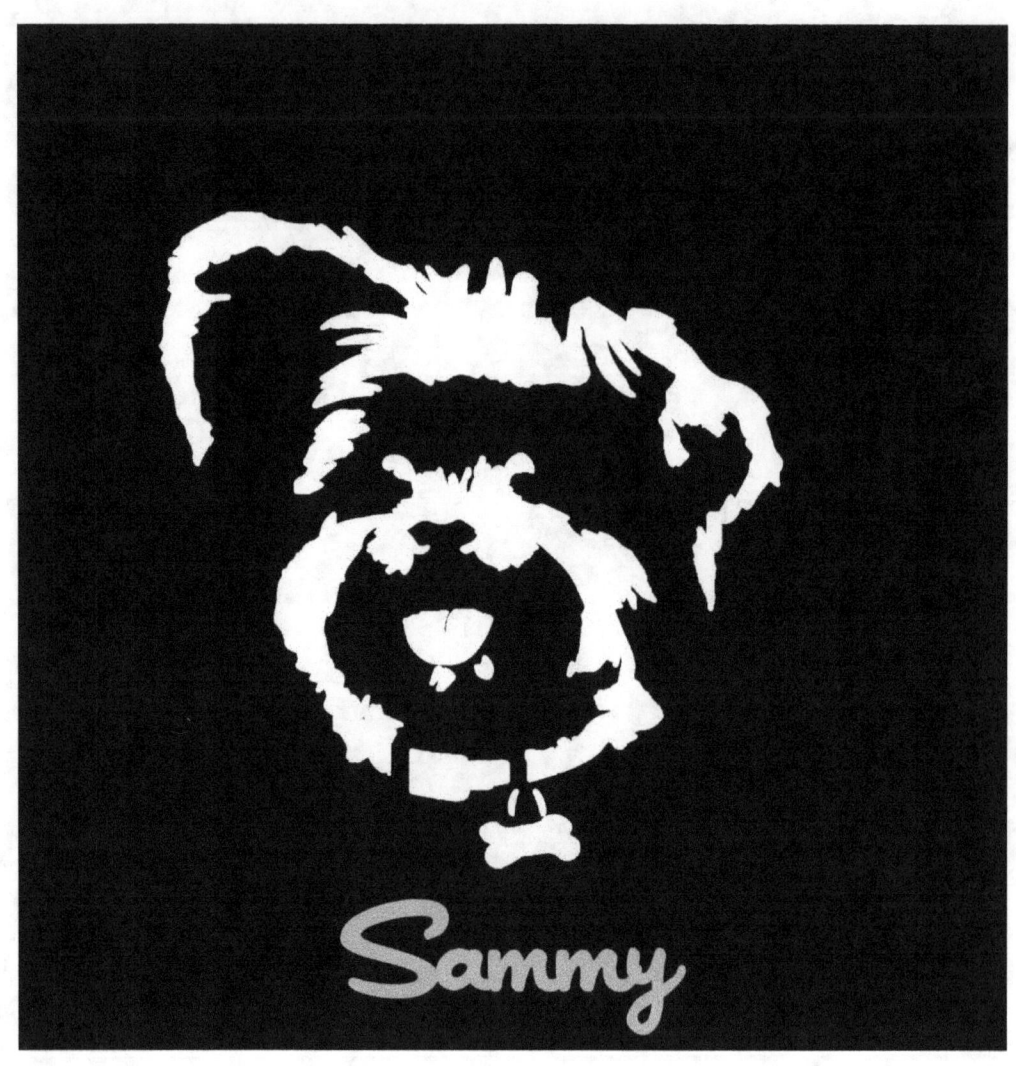

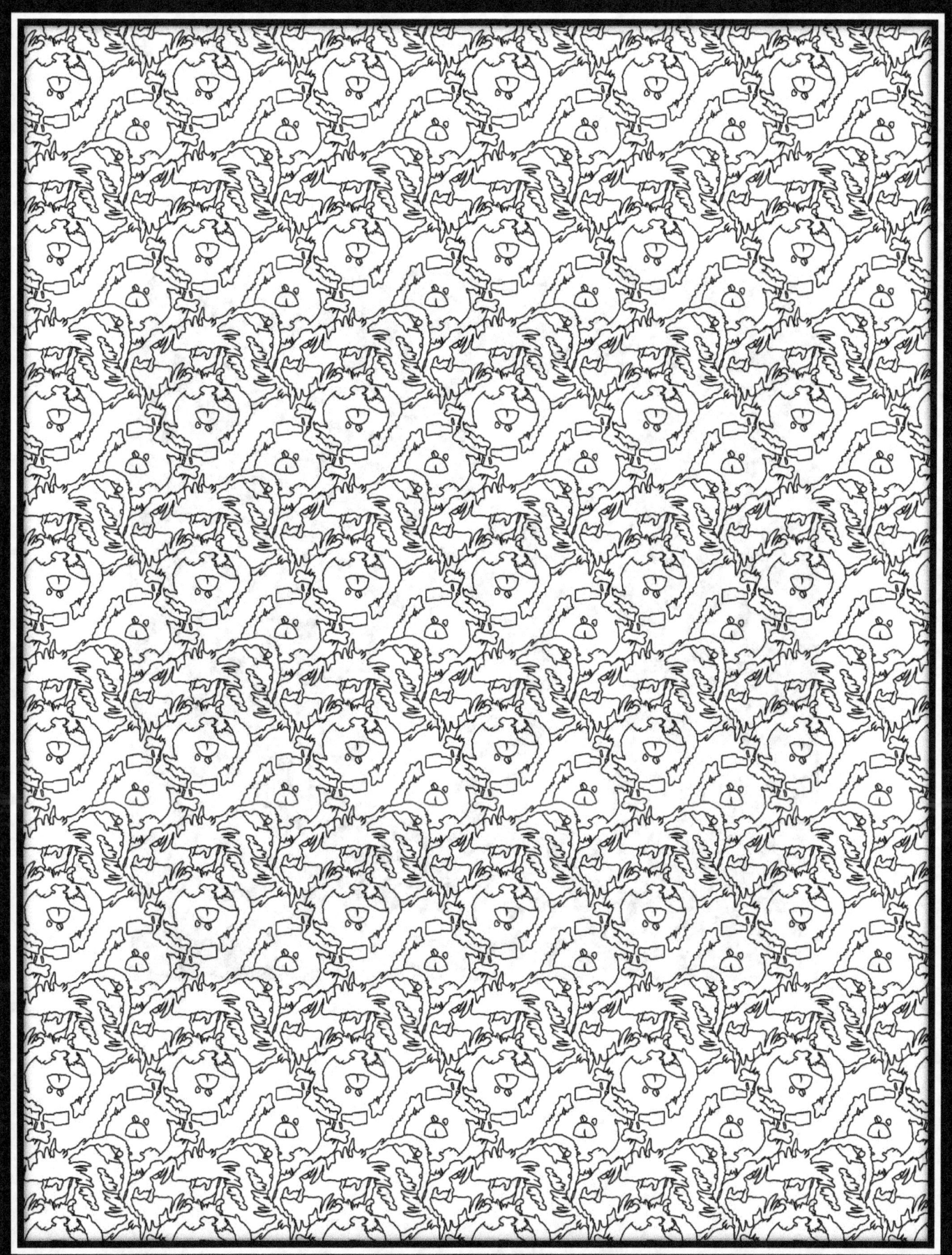

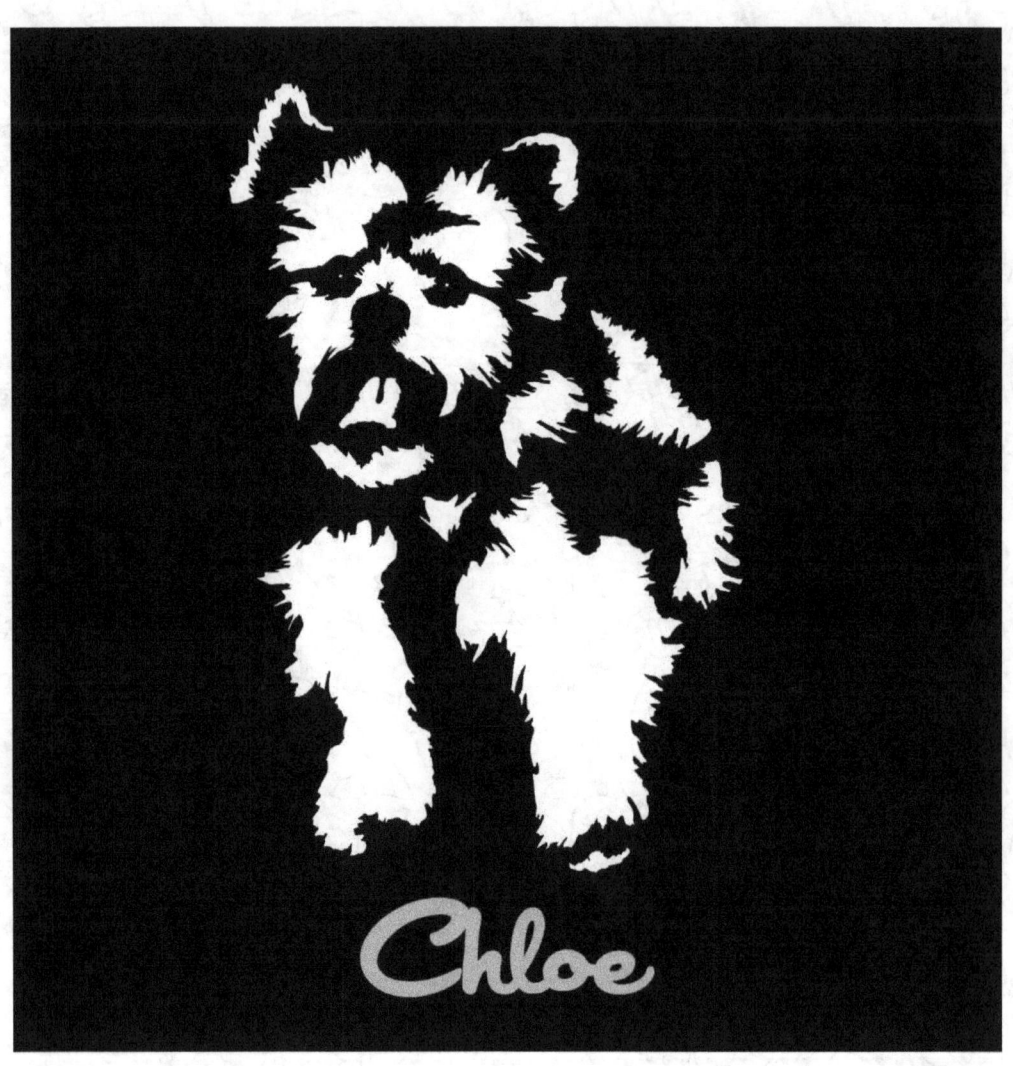

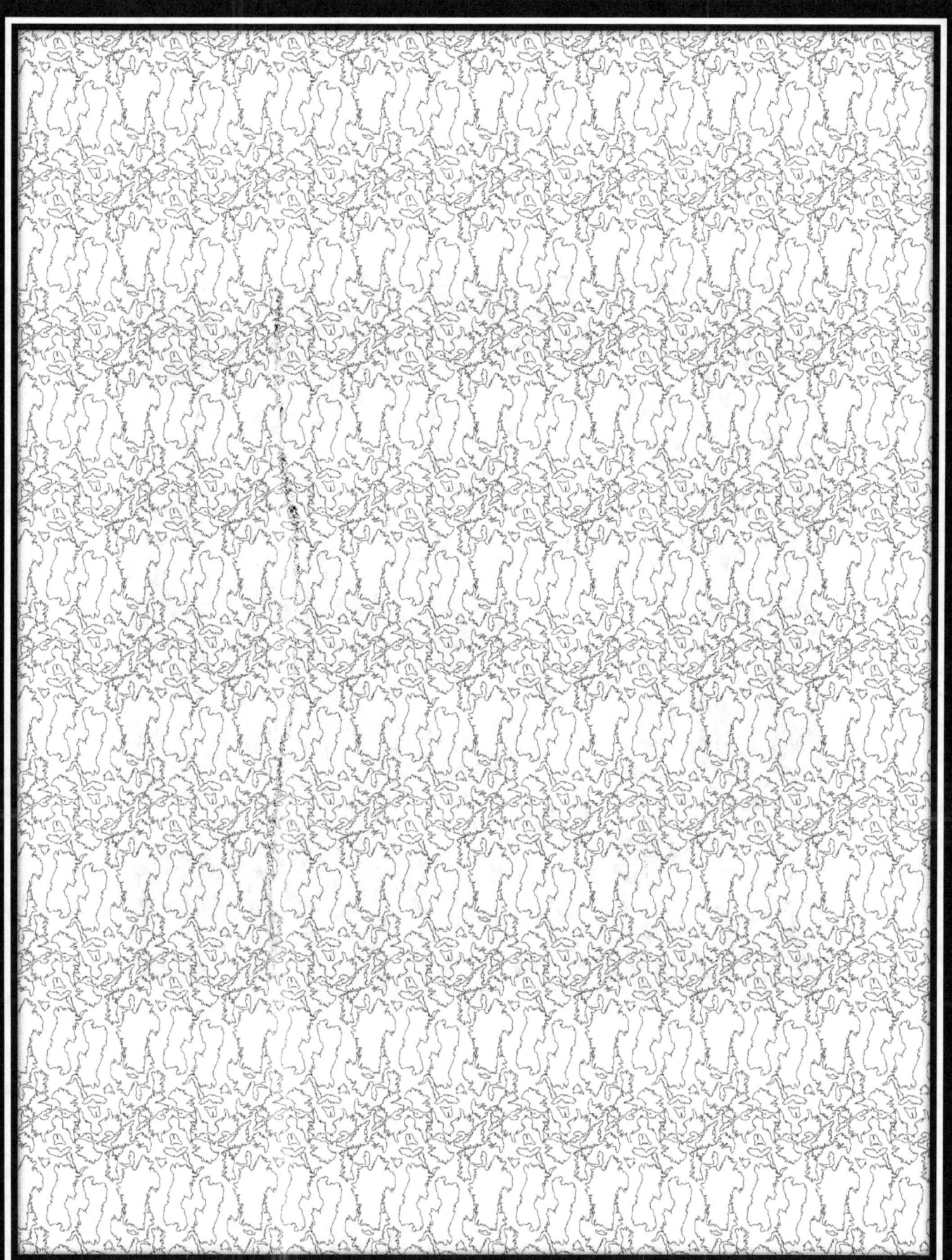

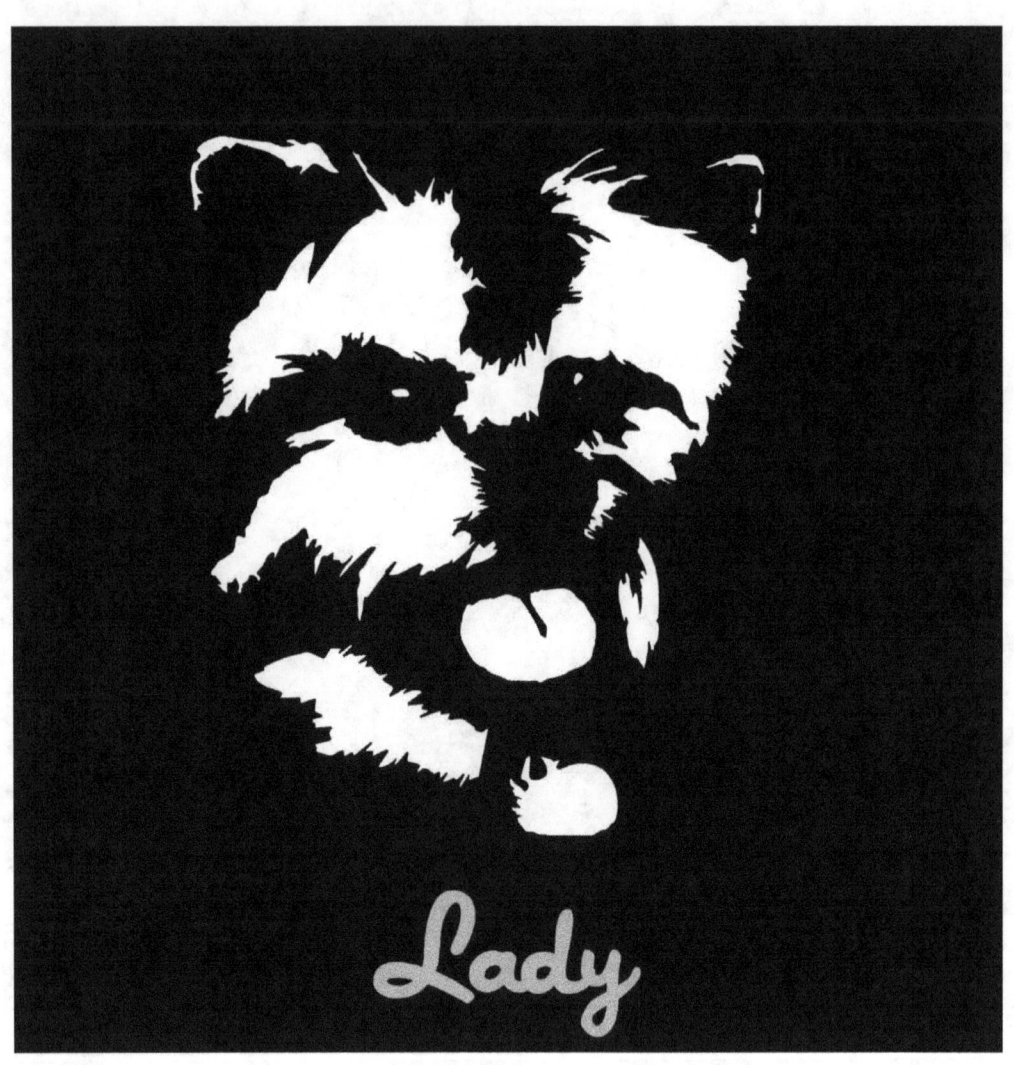

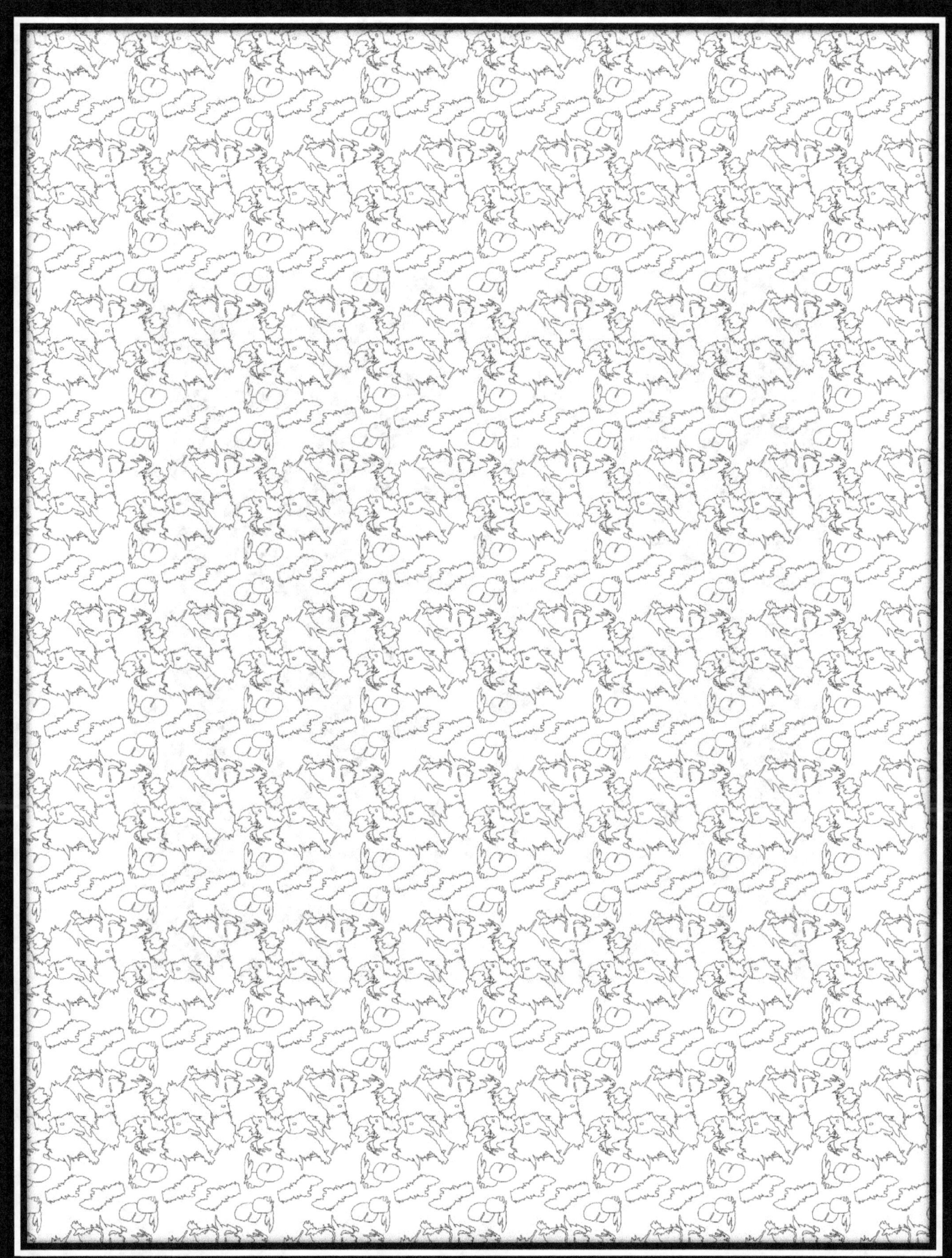

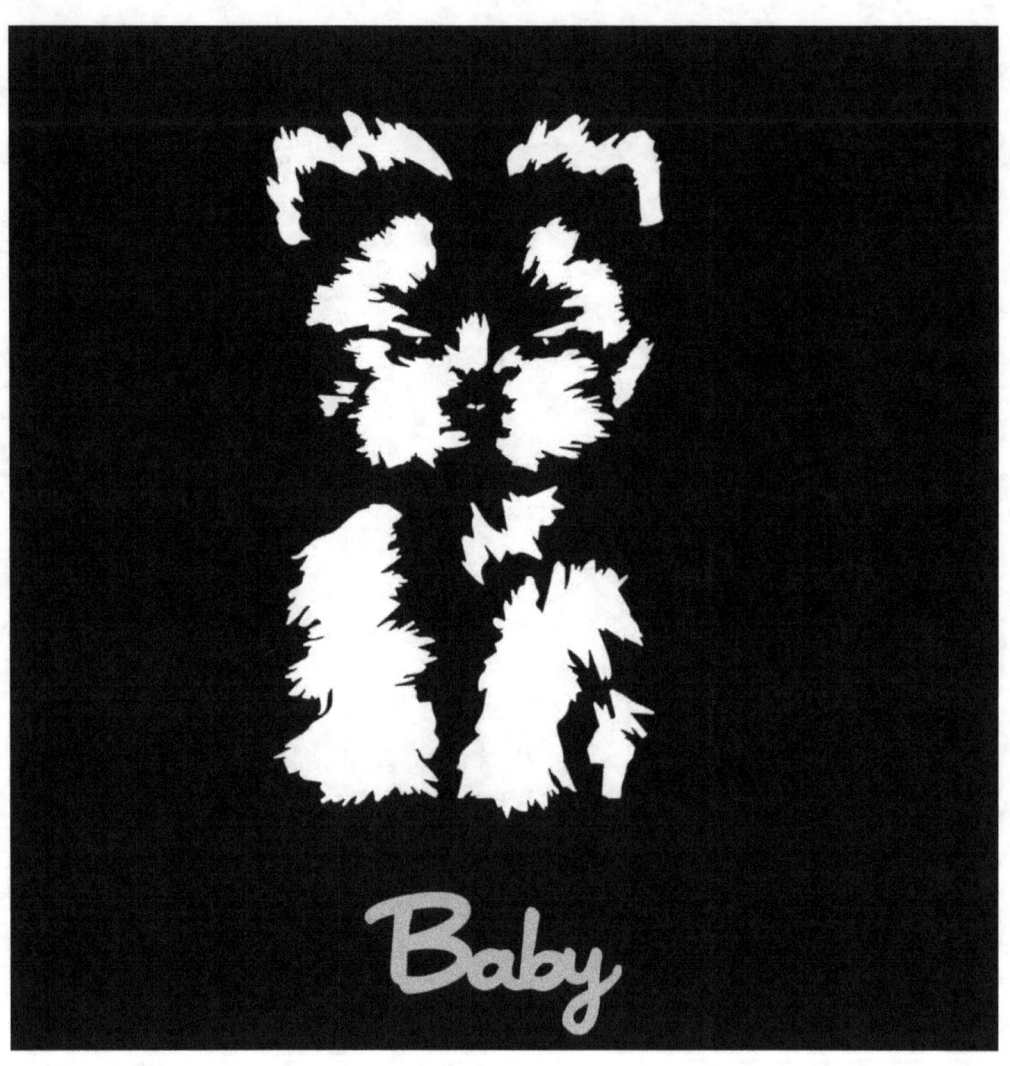

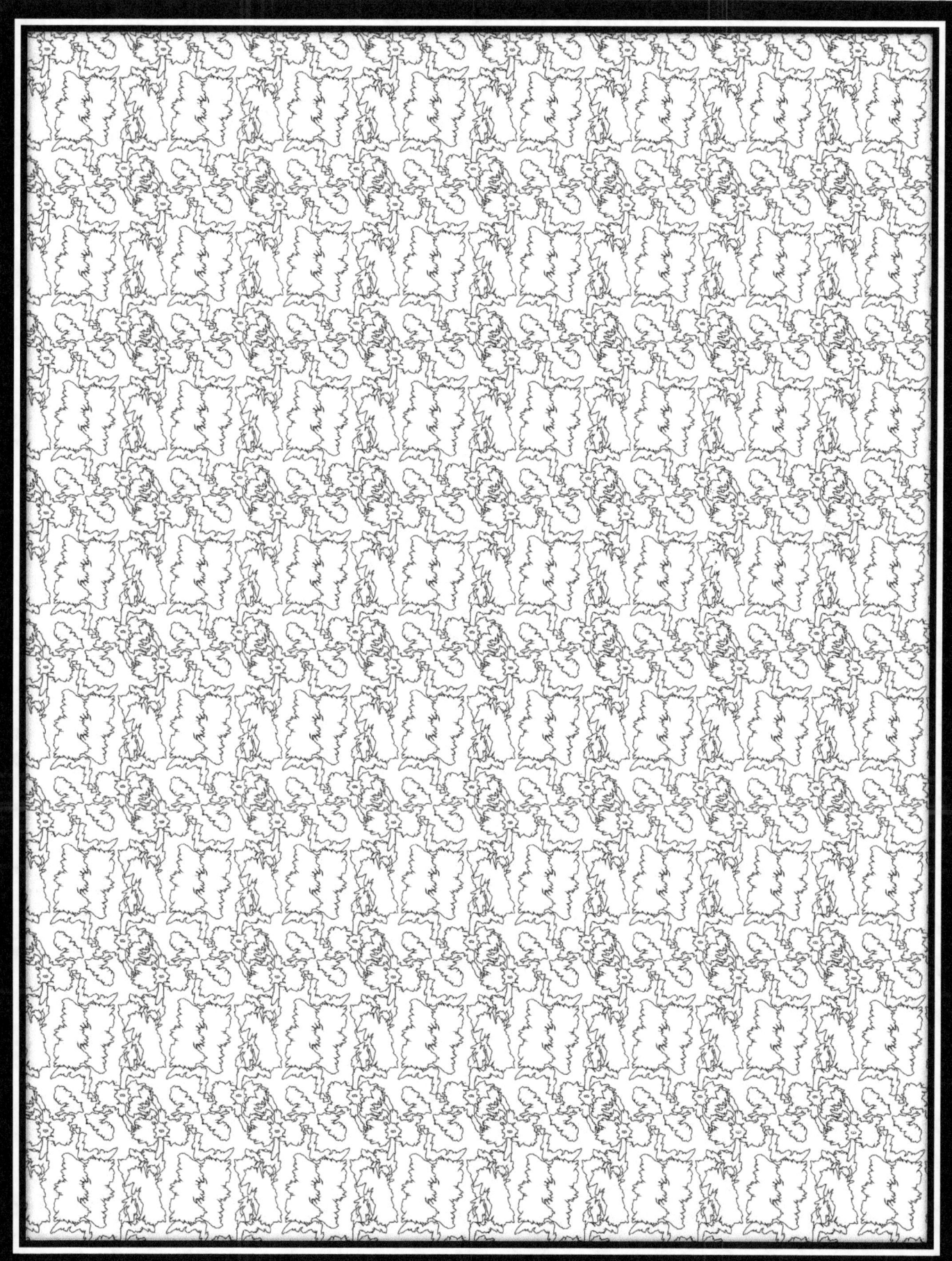

RANDOM PATTERNS

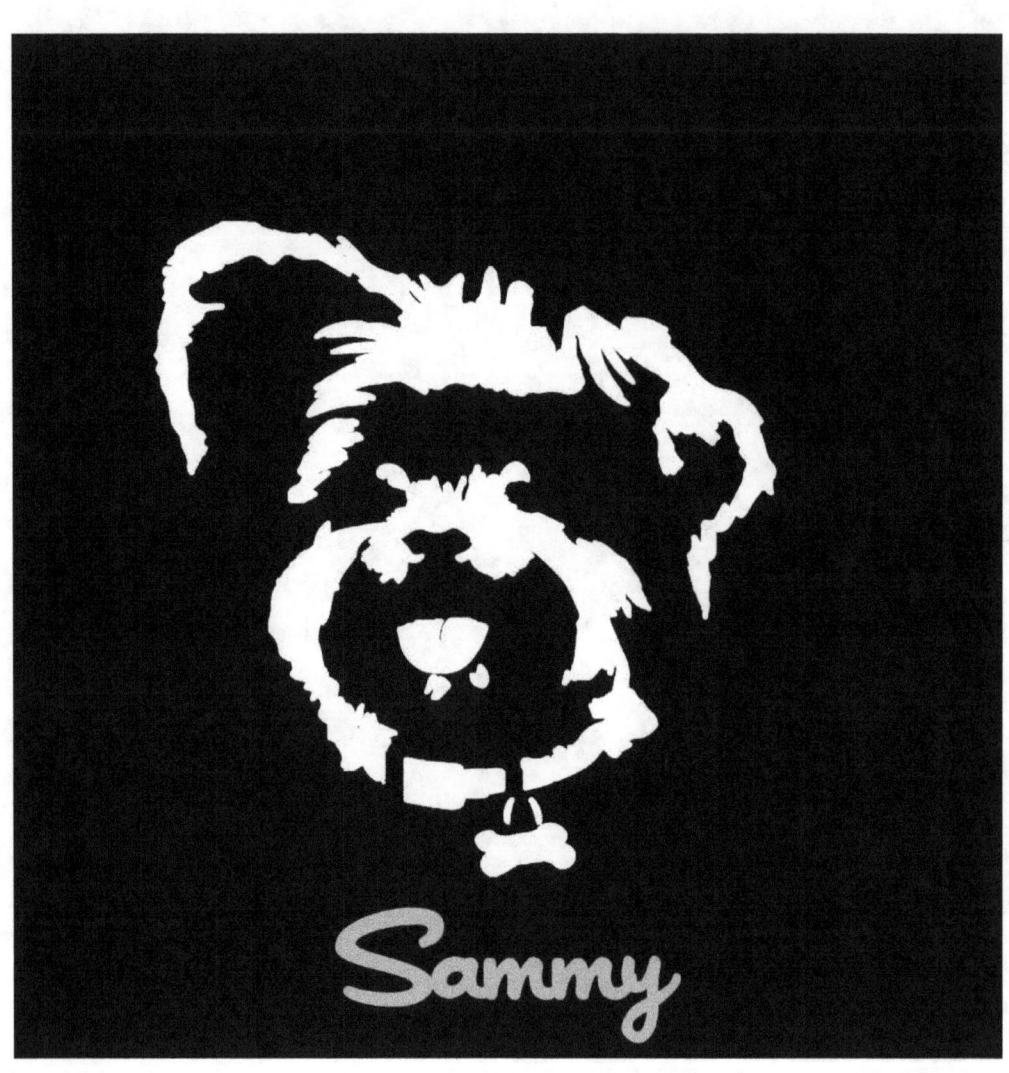

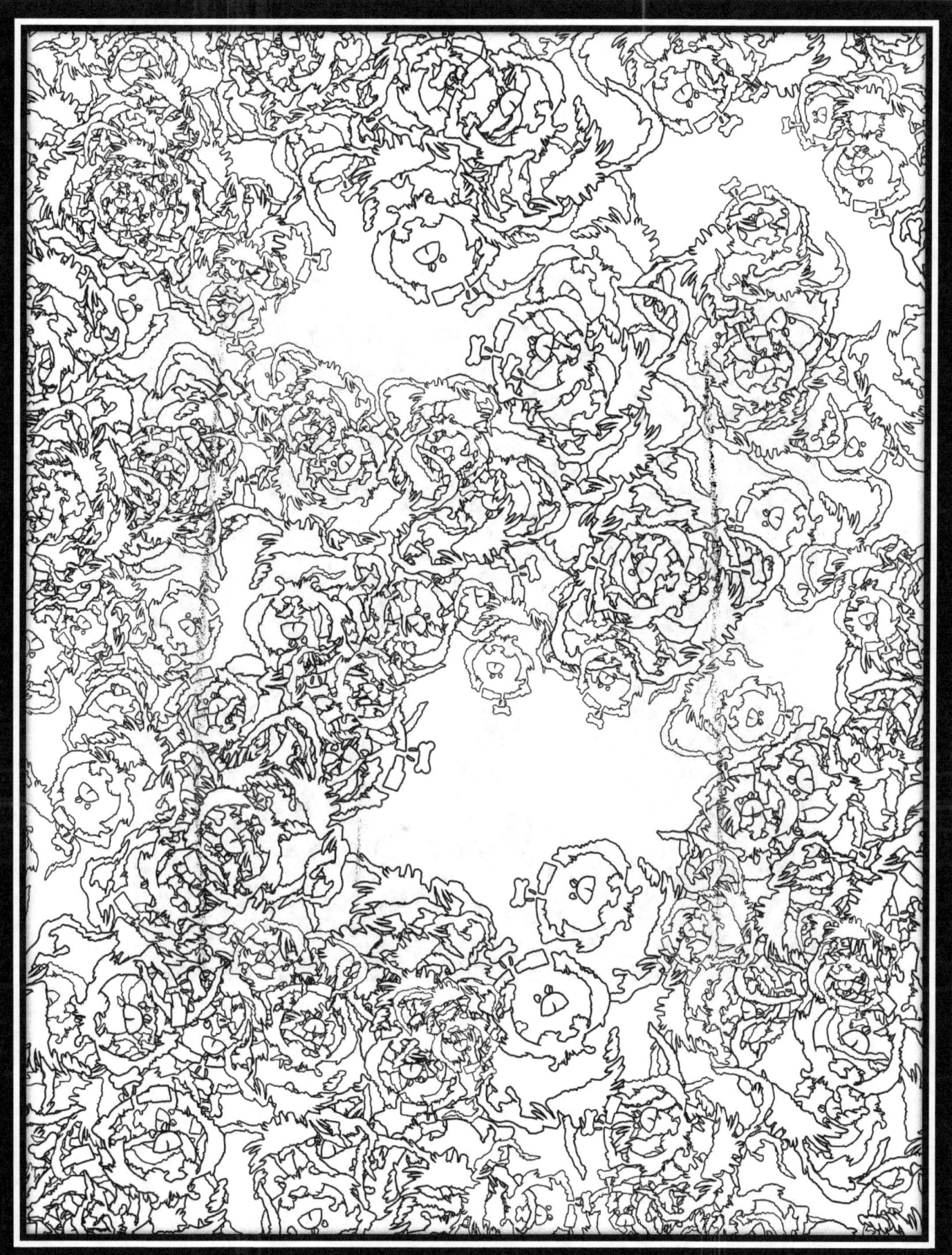

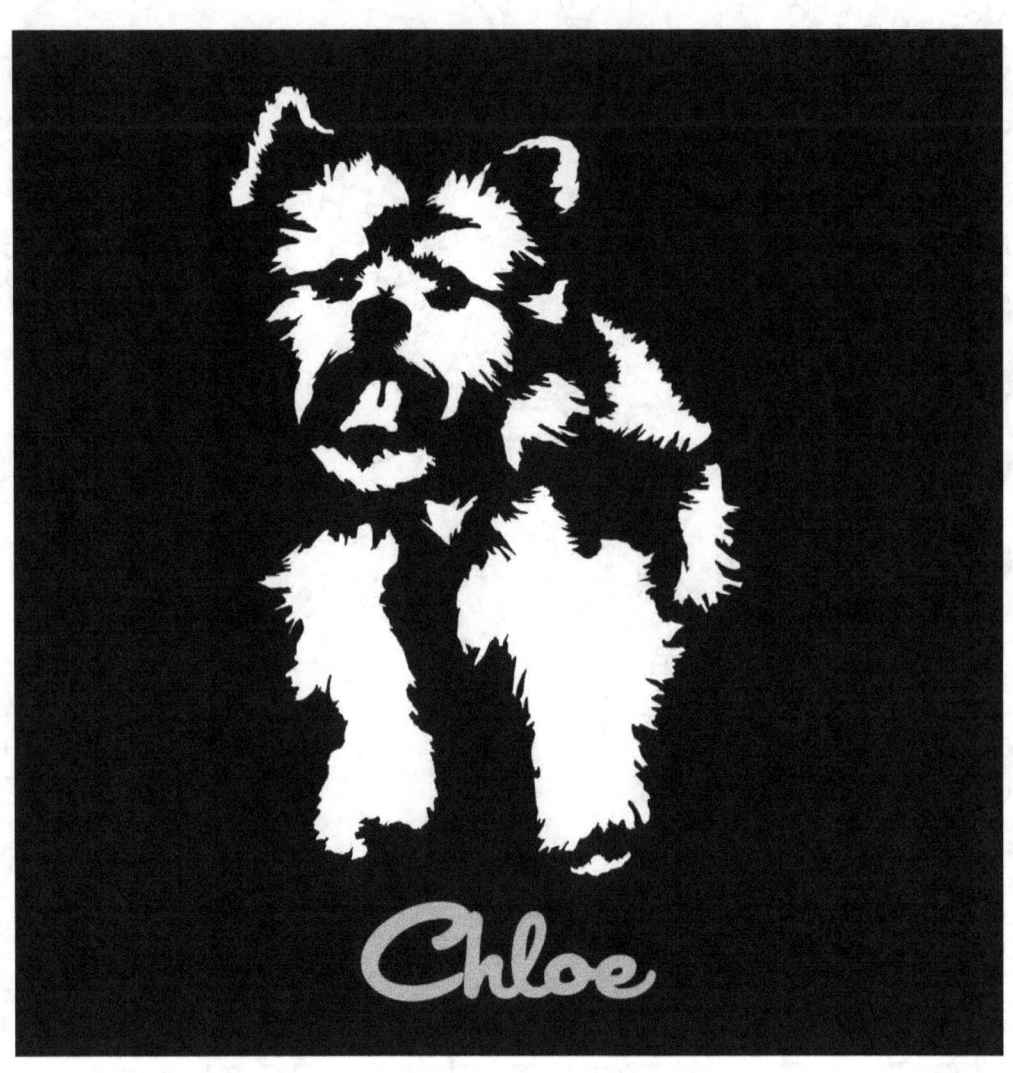

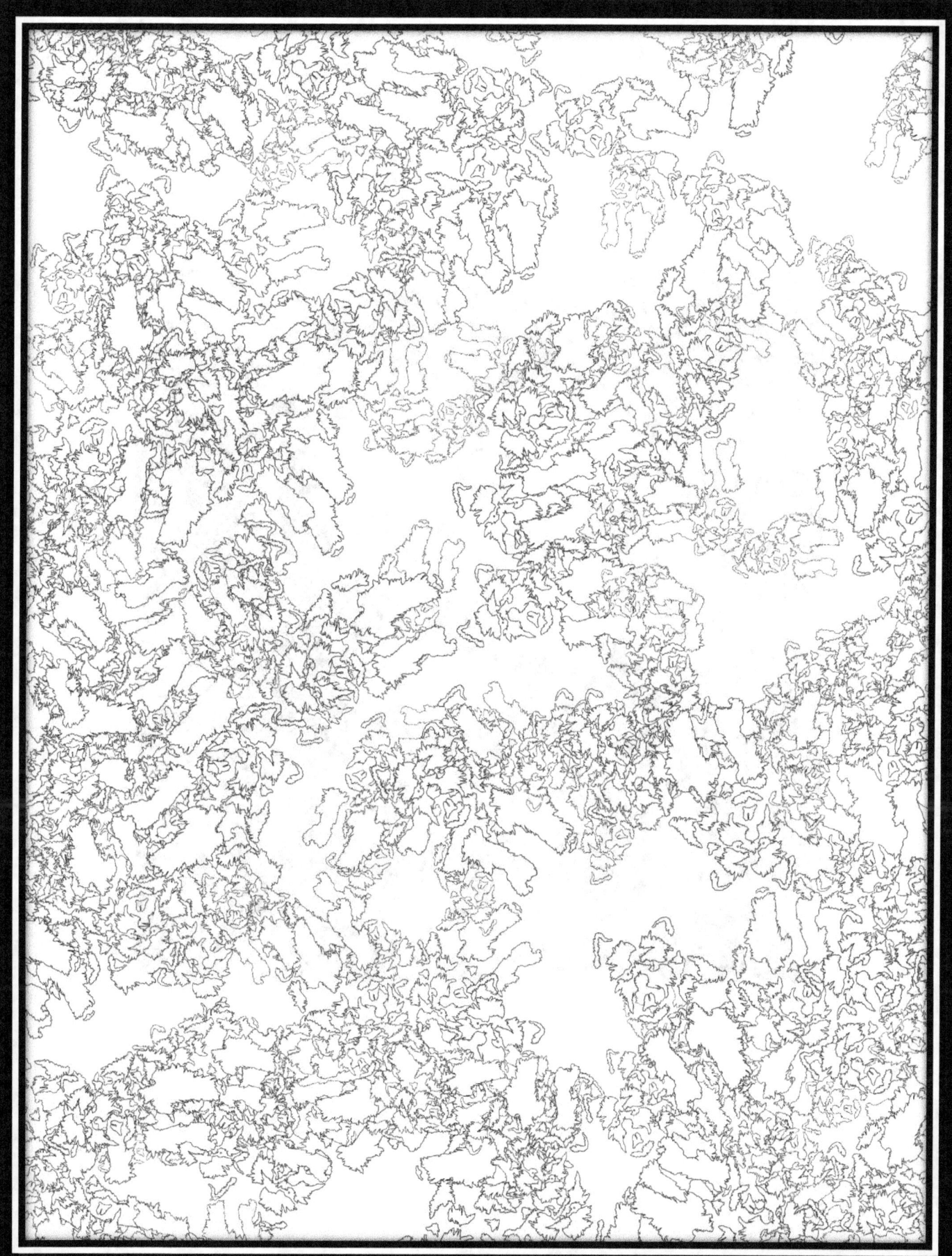

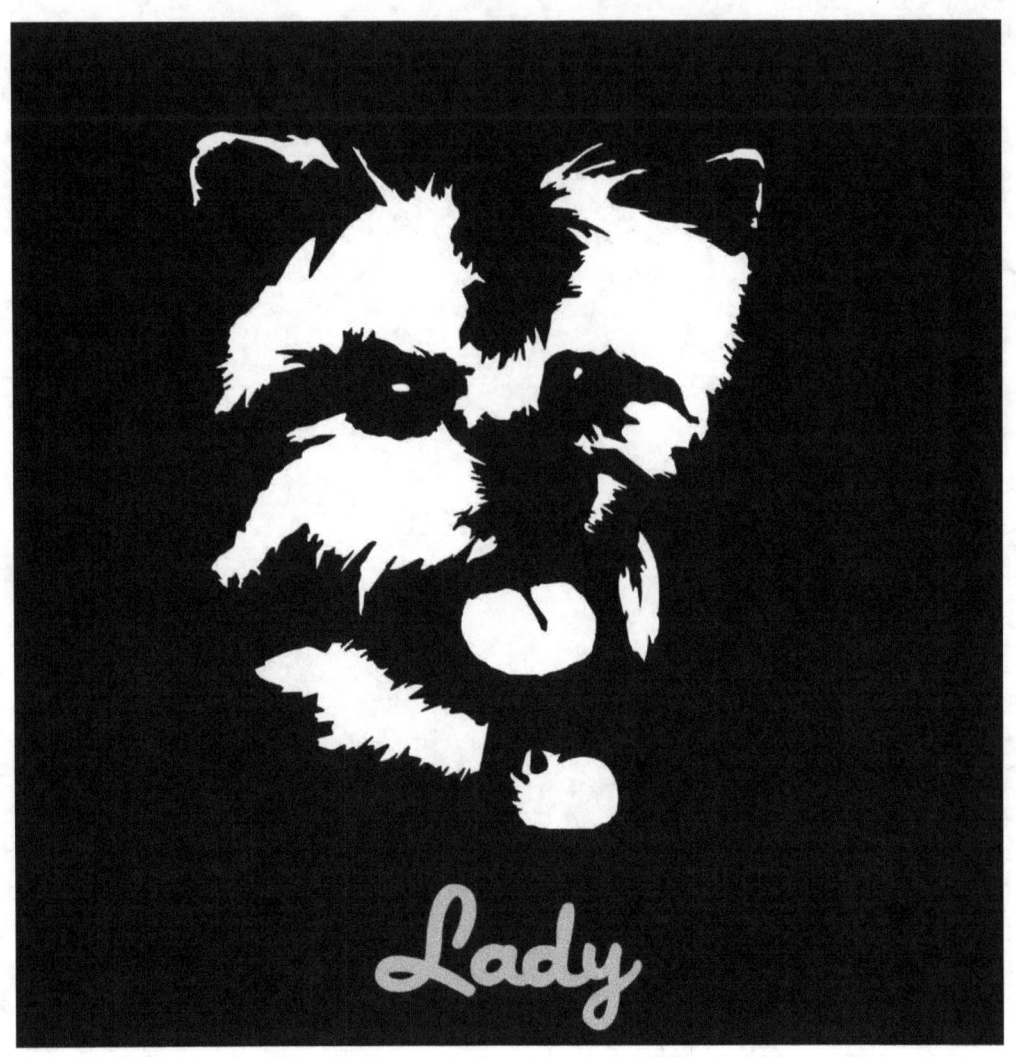

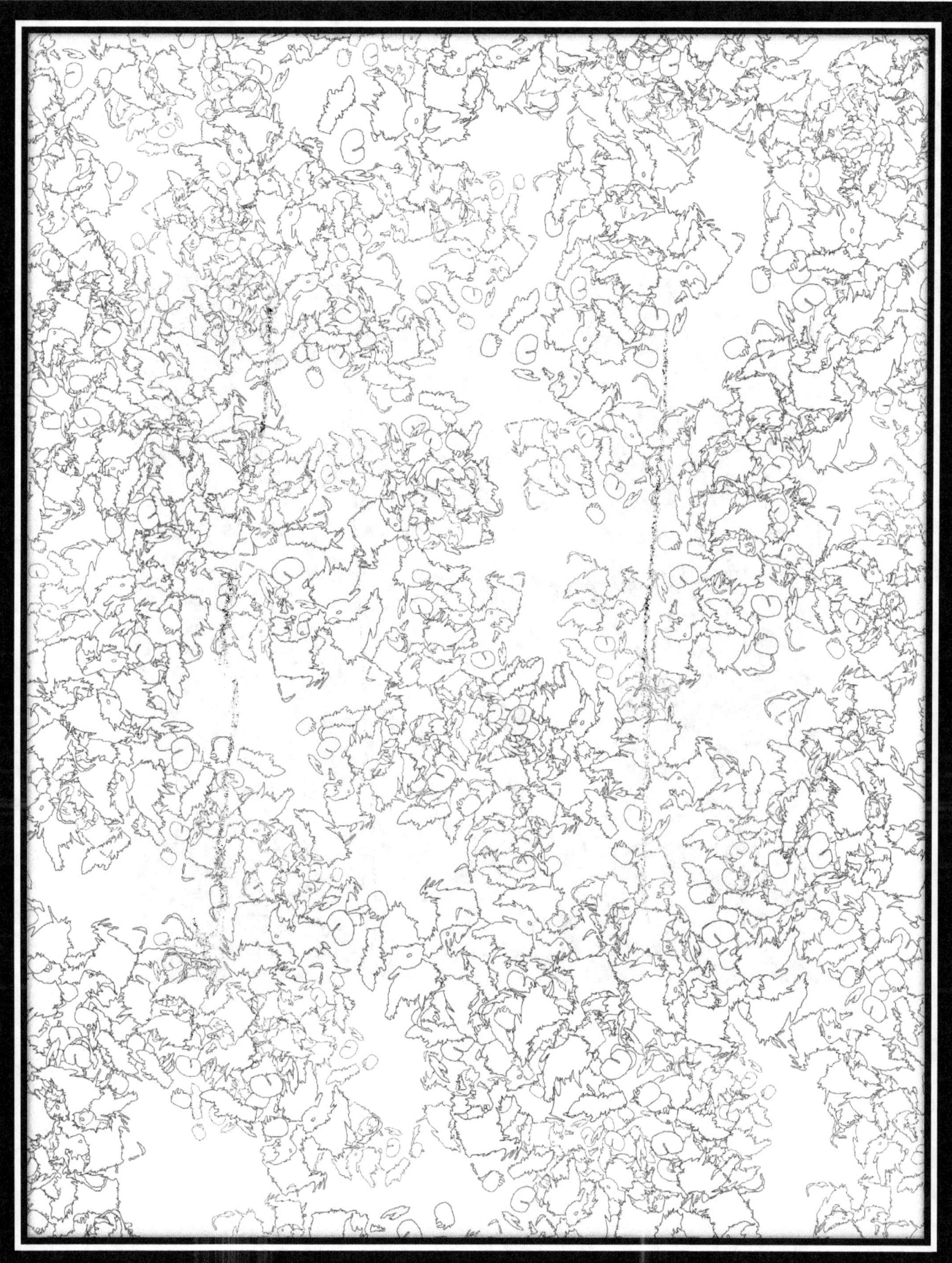

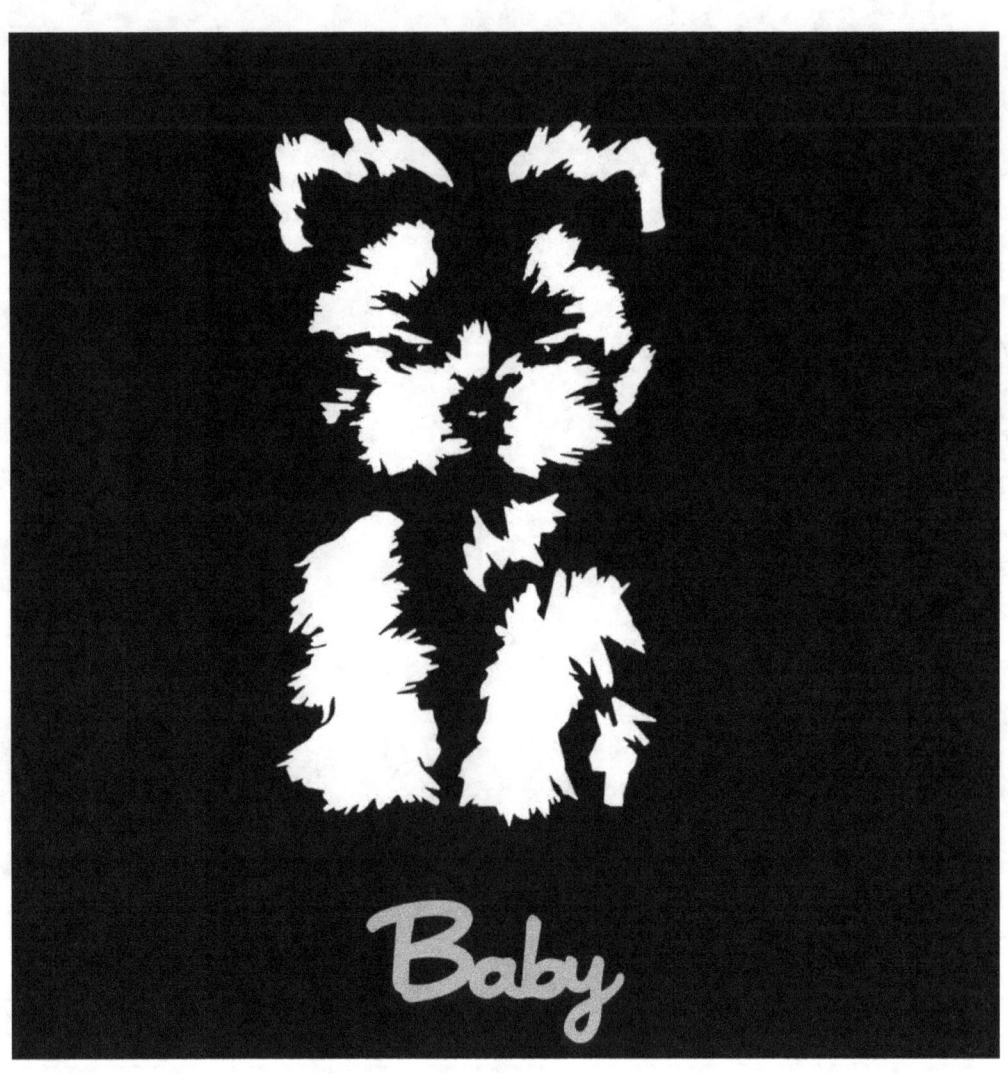

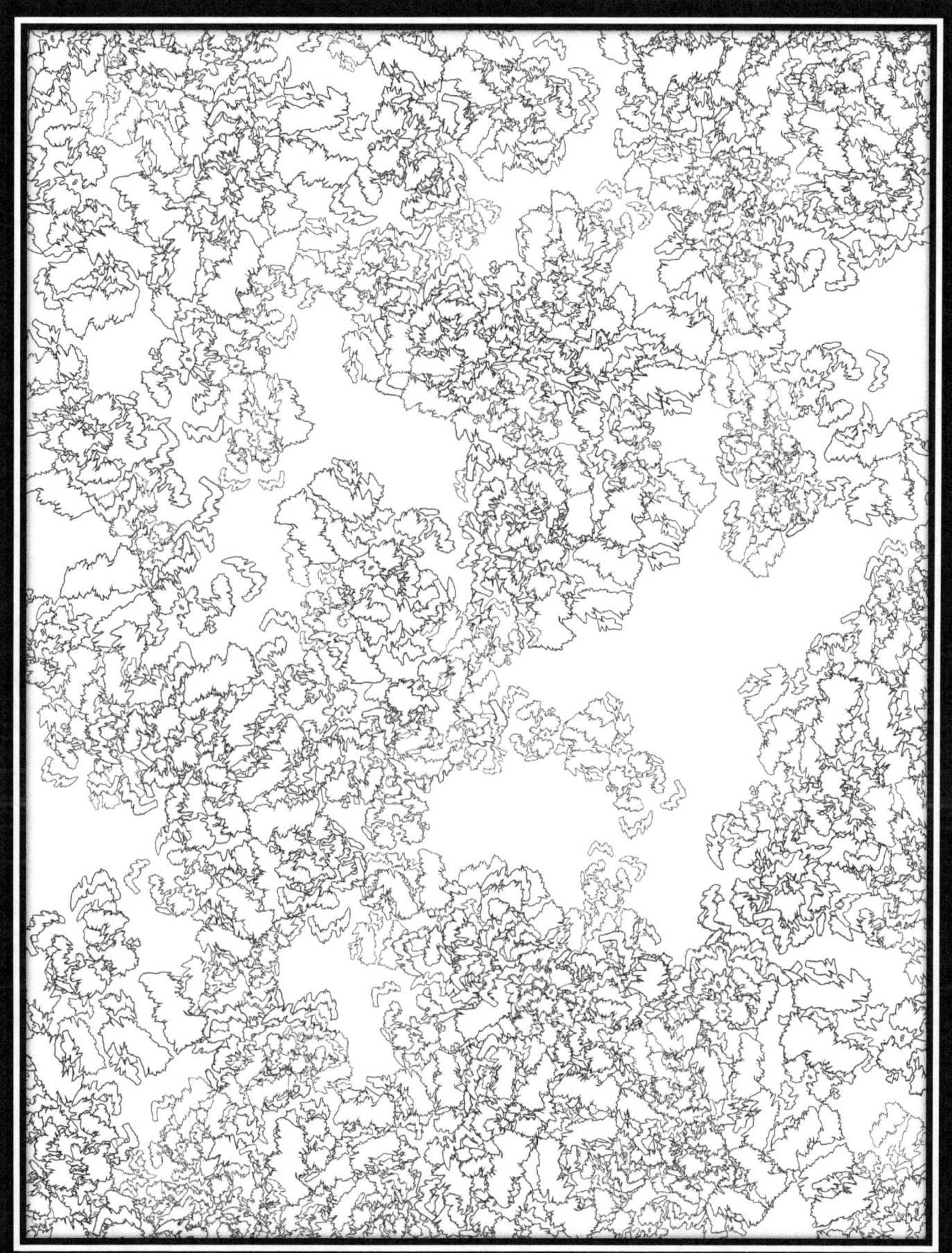

IT'S A YORKIE LIFE

It's a Yorkie Life is a community of Yorkie Lovers big and small.

Join us on our
Website www.itsayorkielife.com, or on
Facebook http://facebook.com/itsayorkielife,
Pinterest http://pinterest.com/itsayorkielife or
Twitter http://twitter.com/itsayorkielife.

www.ingramcontent.com/pod-product-compliance
Lightning Source LLC
Chambersburg PA
CBHW080947170526
45158CB00008B/2400